ADHD
Raising an Explosive
CHILD

The #1 Guide to Helping Parents Understand, Discipline & Empower Kids with Attention Deficit Hyperactivity Disorder to reach Success and Fulfillment with No-Drama

–

Using the Skills of Positive Parenting to Empower Kids with ADHD. Learn Emotional Control Strategies to Help Your Children Self-Regulate and Thrive

by

Anna Wiley

Table of Contents

Chapter 1: An Introduction to ADHD

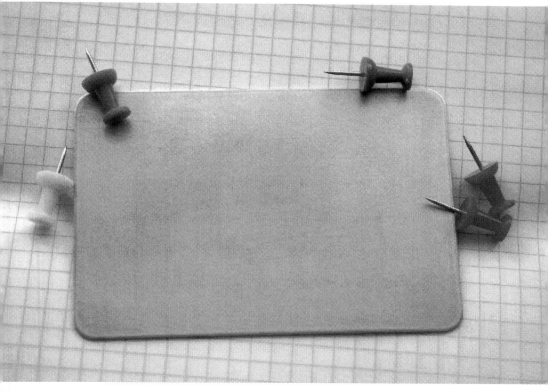

The term ADHD (Attention Deficit Hyperactivity Disorder) gets tossed around quite a lot these days. But truth be told, most people don't really know what it is and why exactly it can be so difficult to live with or to be the parent of a child suffering from ADHD.

Before we dive into parenting a child suffering from ADHD, we must first make a pit-stop and understand what this mental health disorder really means.

Tackling any issue starts with knowing the problem inside and out. This chapter is necessary to help you understand how to raise an "explosive child."

So, without further ado, let's dive in!

What Is ADHD and What Does it Mean?

ADHD is a mental health disorder that causes a mix of hyperactivity and impulsive behaviors. Children are frequently "targeted" by this disorder, but adults are known to suffer from it as well.

ADHD is extremely common to the point that some even dub it to be one of the single most widespread neurodevelopmental disorders of childhood. It's estimated that more than 6.1 million children in the U.S. have been diagnosed with ADHD so far (according to studies released in 2016) (CDC, 2021).

The symptoms can range from mild to severe depending on how many aspects of a person are affected by this disorder. Most times, symptoms tend to vary over time, and adults suffering from ADHD tend to have milder symptoms than they did in childhood. However, adults are suffering from severe ADHD symptoms as well which can impair their daily lives.

Adults suffering from ADHD usually have trouble staying focused at work, in school, and even in their personal lives. They're also more likely to be unemployed or underemployed, face relationship problems, experience a higher rate of divorce than most people, and suffer some other mental health issues as well.

This is precisely why tackling ADHD in childhood is extremely important — it's not just about your peace of mind as a parent but also about the future of your child.

What Does it Mean to Have ADHD?

Living with ADHD can be tough both for the parents and for the children. The good news is that it's possible to live very happily even with ADHD. As you will see in this book, there are plenty of things you can do as a parent to help your child grow healthier, stay more focused, and, generally, be better, both during childhood and as future adults.

So what does it mean to have ADHD?

Let's tackle what it doesn't mean. ADHD is not just a medical name for a child with a bit more energy than usual. All children have plenty of energy and that's a sign they are healthy, both mentally and physically.

However, when the energy is misplaced, too much, and it prevents the child from learning, growing up, and living a life similar to that of other children his/her age, it can become a problem.

In short, having ADHD means the child has trouble paying attention, completing tasks, and following instructions when compared to peers of the same age. It can also mean the child is easily distracted by his/her own thoughts or other people around him/her; doesn't follow through on plans to do a certain

activity because he/she loses interest quickly; and may have difficulty organizing tasks in an orderly manner.

Types of ADHD

Like many other mental health disorders, ADHD comes in different variations:

Predominantly Inattentive Type: People with this version of the disorder are often forgetful, have difficulty focusing on tasks at hand, and may not realize when they need to turn in work. They also tend to lose things easily, misplace items frequently, or be sloppy about their appearance. These symptoms can make them seem lazy or disorganized.

Predominantly Hyperactive-Impulsive Type: This is typically the most severe form of ADHD. People with this condition have a hard time sitting still and may be excessively talkative, fidgety, or impulsive. They are often restless during the day and interrupt others without realizing what they're doing (even if it's making other people mad).

Combined type: Those diagnosed with this specific type of ADHD have both symptoms of inattentiveness and hyperactivity/impulsivity.

Comprehending ADHD

One of the sad truths about ADHD is that, like other mental health disorders (depression, anxiety, and so on), it is not fully understood. We do understand quite a lot about it at this point. Though we know enough to build treatment schemes and help both children and adults suffering from this attention disorder. At the end of the day though, the complex, intrinsic mechanisms and psychopathology of ADHD are not fully understood.

ADHD Types of Symptoms and Characteristics of a Child with ADHD

Keep in mind that no mental health disorder should ever be diagnosed at home. If you notice any of the following symptoms, you should definitely consult with a specialist for a diagnosis.

So, what are the symptoms and characteristics of a child with ADHD (Health-line, 2020)?

- Hyperactivity
- Impulsiveness
- Inattention/disorganization
- Excessive daydreaming or talking
- Self-focused behavior
- Interrupting
- Having trouble waiting for their turn
- Fidgeting
- Emotional turmoil
- Cannot play quietly
- Frequently doesn't finish tasks
- Avoiding mental effort of any kind

While these are not *all* symptoms a child with ADHD might experience, they are among the more common ones, so you should definitely keep them in mind.

ADHD Etiological Classification

In a traditional understanding of the disorder, ADHD is caused by a dopamine deficiency; it's a decreased blood flow in the prefrontal cortex and cerebellum part of the brain, as well as the ganglia, which has an important role in creating dopamine.

ADHD can be triggered by an array of causes and, as such, scientists have categorized this disorder according to its cause (which is referred to as an "etiological classification").

Here are the main categories you should be aware of here (Kessler, 2021):

- Inattentive ADHD, caused by dopamine deficiency and insufficient activity in the prefrontal cortex.
- Overfocused ADHD, which is caused by dopamine and serotonin deficiencies, as well as overactive anterior cingulate gyrus.
- Temporal lobe ADHD, which is caused by too much activity in the limbic part of the brain and by decreased activity in the prefrontal cortex (regardless of whether the child is focusing on a task or at rest).
- Ring of Fire ADHD, caused by too much activity in the entire brain, including the cerebral cortex and other areas.
- Anxious ADHD, which is a combination of anxiety and ADD and is caused by high activity in the basal ganglia area of the brain.

Each of these types of ADHD comes with its own set of symptoms and specific treatment, but we will get into this a little later on in the book.

The ADHD Brain

While we cannot fully understand what happens in the human brain when it is affected by certain disorders (ADHD included), we do have a very good idea of how the brain reacts to these problems.

In the case of ADHD, it is believed that the brain has a problem with its dopamine production which causes it to be less able to tune out distractions.

Dopamine is very tightly linked with a neurotransmitter called norepinephrine, and when there is an issue in its production, the dopamine levels are affected as well. Since dopamine is the neurotransmitter dealing with the pleasure center of the brain, an imbalance in its levels can translate into a series of symptoms many of which can fall under the ADHD umbrella.

It is not exactly clear how ADHD develops and multiple theories have been raised.

One theory of ADHD's cause states that certain connections within the frontal lobe make an individual more susceptible to impulsive behavior, including hyperactivity or lack of focus on one task.

Other theories state that when the brain suffers from ADHD, a person has less of an inhibitory response to stimuli in the environment and is unable to filter out what it considers unimportant.

For some people with ADHD to focus or concentrate on something without being distracted by other things, they need more stimulus than others.

Some studies have found that ADHD is largely hereditary and that there might be a genetic link. Children and siblings of someone who suffers from ADHD are more likely to develop the disorder as well (NHS, 2021). Of course, this is not always the case, but research shows there is a higher likelihood in this direction.

What's the Difference Between ADD and ADHD?

When you start reading about Attention Deficit Hyperactivity Disorder, you might get confused by the fact that you will see it shortened to both ADD and ADHD. In reality, there is no difference between the two. ADHD is the unanimously accepted current version of this disorder's name. ADD is an outdated version of the same name, mostly used to describe inattentive-type ADHD (but

since more discoveries have been made in this field, we now know that this is not the only type of ADHD there is).

In the following chapters, we will look more in-depth at a variety of topics related to ADHD, including symptomatology, causes, and how to help your child if they have been diagnosed with this disorder.

Chapter 2: How to Identify the Symptoms of ADHD in a Child

Every child with ADHD is different — the symptoms they experience can be wildly different as well. Learning how to spot the first symptoms and when to call for the services of a medical professional are crucial steps in parenting a child with Attention Deficit Hyperactivity Disorder — precisely because they will help you better manage the situation in the future.

In this chapter, we will dig more into the topic of ADHD symptoms and how parents can spot them early (or at least as early as possible).

ADHD Symptoms at Every Age

ADHD diagnosis can sometimes be tricky because a child has to show six (or more) symptoms, from the list we will share with you below, for more than six months. Usually, the diagnosis of ADHD can be made at any time between the age of four and the age of 16. If you suspect that your child may have ADHD, the child should be observed closely for symptoms throughout adolescents. The frequency of symptoms is just as important as noting when the symptoms first appeared and how the child is affected when you are seeking a diagnosis.

There are two large categories of symptoms that can help you identify ADHD in a child. The first category is related to inattention while the second one is related to hyperactivity, both are essential components of ADHD.

Inattention-related symptoms include trouble with the following:

- Paying attention to details or making careless mistakes
- Focusing on tasks or even during playtime
- Listening when an adult is speaking to them directly, even when the adult is in a position of authority (like a parent or a teacher)
- Following instructions on tasks, homework, or chores
- Organizing their tasks and activities
- Completing tasks that require them to focus or devote mental effort for longer periods
- Keeping track of their things (school supplies, phone, glasses, and so on)
- Avoiding distractions
- Remembering things when they are running a daily activity

Hyperactivity-related symptoms include having trouble with the following:

- Fidgeting, tapping their hands or their feet, squirming, and so on
- Standing up and getting away from their seat in situations where they should remain seated (such as at school or in the church)
- Running and climbing in places and situations they shouldn't be doing this
- The ability to take part in certain activities quietly
- Feeling like they are permanently on-the-go
- Talking excessively
- Answering rapidly before the question is even spelled out
- Interrupting conversations and games

Most of these symptoms are seen frequently in children and teenagers with ADHD. However, as mentioned above, one or two of these symptoms, popping up sporadically, do not necessarily lead to a diagnosis of ADHD. Furthermore, every child or teenager will behave differently and there are, of course, differences between how children and teenagers behave (e.g. teens might be more inclined towards reckless behavior).

Adult ADHD is rarely diagnosed and there's insufficient research in this area. This is mostly because, with ADHD being a developmental disorder, it is assumed that an adult with ADHD will have already been diagnosed in childhood. Generally, by the age of 25, about 15% of the adults diagnosed with ADHD as children will still have the full range of symptoms and 65% will experience symptoms that affect their daily lives (NHS, 2021).

In adults, ADHD can cause the following symptoms:

- Inability to focus on tasks
- Trouble remaining organized and completing necessary daily chores such as making the bed, doing dishes, or washing clothes
- Impatience with people who are slower or less articulate than they are
- Difficulty reading social cues from others (e.g., missing sarcasm)
- Starting new tasks before finishing old ones
- Frequently losing items
- Having a hard time sitting still for long periods
- Dealing with forgetfulness and impulsiveness
- Inability to listen when someone is talking, blurting out inappropriate comments, or answers before the speaker finishes

A child will show symptoms like these:

- Poor academic results at school due to lack of focus on their tasks
- Behavior problems at school (e.g., not staying in their seat)
- Trouble getting along with others, including family members and friends
- Impatience with themselves or sluggish movements when they do something without being motivated to do it; trouble doing things that need to be done quickly such as assembling a toy or dressing for the day
- Interrupting others and blurting out responses

- Acting without thinking
- Trouble following instructions or routines that are laid out in a logical order
- Experiencing mood swings, a quick temper, and irritability
- Inability to deal with stress

Some adults might not have any symptoms at all while some may only experience a few of them that don't interfere too heavily in their lives. Adults might also be diagnosed when ADHD is suspected for either themselves or their children because there's no way to tell if someone has ADHD just by looking at them. The process can involve the following: physical exams, lab tests, imaging scans like X-rays and MRIs; questionnaires, and interviews with adults, parents, and teachers (in the case of adults who are still in school/ higher education, for example). There is no physical test for ADHD, but tests may be used to rule out other causes.

ADHD Symptoms in Children

In essence, there are three main (major) groups of symptoms displayed by children with ADHD: inattention, hyperactivity, and impulsivity. That doesn't mean that a child with a lot of energy or with a more impulsive character is automatically diagnosed with ADHD. As mentioned before, multiple criteria have to be met for someone (child or not) to be diagnosed with this disorder.

Many other characteristics can contribute to the diagnosis, such as difficulty sitting still or playing quietly; avoid tasks requiring sustained attention (reading for more than five minutes); and fidgeting. Fidgety behavior may include squirming in their seat when they have been asked to do something, tapping items on the desk repetitively, as well as shaking their head, or wiggling in place.

For more information on the general ADHD symptoms (frequently seen in children), please refer to what has been mentioned in the first part of this chapter.

ADHD Symptoms and Your Child's Education

Since on many occasions ADHD comes with a lack of focus, it can affect a child's education. Both in the classroom and at home, they may have difficulty following instructions or remembering things that were just said. This can cause them to lose interest in their work and become easily distracted by what is going on around them.

If ADHD is not being treated correctly or at all, the symptoms in children can make it difficult for them to function properly both inside of the classroom and outside of it.

Additionally, children with ADHD are at risk of growing up to be adults who don't perform well academically or at work, as well as have issues in their personal lives (such as in their personal relationships or engage in risky sexual practices, for example). Moreover, research also shows that ADHD patients can frequently show comorbid mental health disorders (such as Bipolar Disorder, for example) (Usami, 2016).

This is not to say that all children diagnosed with ADHD will have these issues. It's also not meant to scare you as a parent. ADHD can be managed. Being aware of further issues is important precisely because it will help you take action now.

To help manage ADHD in children, it is important to understand what triggers symptoms. For example, when a child with ADHD enters an unfamiliar setting (such as a new classroom), they may experience significant difficulties managing their time and concentrating on the work at hand.

It's also common for them to get bored easily or distracted by things around them, and thus, lose concentration in class. Therefore, they might have trouble keeping track of what was said in lectures or following directions.

Your child needs to be taught by professionals who know how to handle ADHD. Some techniques can help a child with ADHD stay more focused, including:

- Delivering information in tidbits
- Making sure the child is seated so that all distractions are avoided
- Creating worksheets and tests that have fewer items on them
- Helping the child organize themselves (such as by providing them with a notebook with three pockets: homework assignments, completed homework, and messages for the parents

These are just some of the techniques that should be incorporated in the education of a child diagnosed with ADHD. To someone on the outside, they might not seem like a lot, but it is precisely these kinds of small things that can make a major difference in the life of someone with ADHD.

Other Symptoms of ADHD

As mentioned earlier, every person with ADHD is different. Although there might be different pathologies as to how this disorder develops, most of those

diagnosed with ADHD show similar symptoms that fall into the spectrum we have already mentioned in the first section of this chapter.

In addition to the symptomatology itself, it is also important to keep in mind that ADHD symptoms can sometimes be mistaken with symptoms of other disorders, such as

- Sensory processing disorders
- Autism
- Bipolar disorder
- Low blood sugar
- Hearing problems

Of course, symptoms of ADHD should also not be mistaken with kids just being... kids. Only a medical specialist can help you find an actual diagnosis, so do make sure you visit one if you think your child might show symptoms of Attention Deficit Hyperactive Disorder.

Chapter 3: Possible Causes of ADHD

If your child has been diagnosed with ADHD, why might be a question you ask yourself (and perhaps quite often). The sad truth is that there's no clear cause of ADHD and that this disorder might develop as a result of multiple different causes. Research is not conclusive in this respect, but staying informed will help you manage your child's diagnosis better.

For this reason, we are dedicating the third chapter of this book to exploring the potential causes of ADHD.

Let's take a closer look at this!

Genetics

Research shows that genetics can play an important role in the development of ADHD. In fact, in many cases, it's found that children who have a sibling with ADHD will also be diagnosed with this disorder themselves (around 30% to 50%). The risk is even higher when both parents are affected by ADHD as

well - they can pass on those genes to their children and cause them future problems because they are more likely to inherit an ADHD diagnosis.

This does not necessarily mean that if a parent has ADHD the child is automatically going to have the same diagnosis. However, the risk is higher. If you have been diagnosed with ADHD in the past, genetics might have played a role in the development of the same disorder in your child (Faraone, Larsson, 2019).

Brain Development

Scientists have found that the brain develops much slower in children with ADHD and their brains get to a point where they are catching up later on when compared to other children. For this reason, many times it's not until age nine or ten before doctors can really diagnose these patients as having ADHD.

As mentioned previously, research is not conclusive in terms of what causes ADHD. However, more recent studies show that there is, indeed, a neurological basis for the development of ADHD. More specifically, studies have shown that certain parts of the brain are smaller in people with ADHD whereas others are larger.

At the same time, scientists have also learned that a specific type of neurological development that leads to ADHD can also predict when the disorder will be normalized (Singer, 2007).

Environmental Factors

While environmental factors are usually not considered to be actual causes of ADHD, they can be significant risk factors. Some of these factors include:

- Food additives and diet
- Lead contamination
- Cigarette exposure
- Smoking during pregnancy
- A low birth weight
- The neurological basis for ADHD

Other causes for the development of ADHD include brain damage and epilepsy. Furthermore, ADHD in adults can also be related to neurological issues that appear during their development.

How can you prevent your child from having ADHD?

Well, there's nothing specific you can do.

There are many ways to help children to avoid an ADHD diagnosis (or, better said, to avoid the progression of this disorder), but scientists have found that the best way is by giving them a good start in life as early as possible.

The earlier they get therapy and interventions for this disorder, the chances of developing it later on down the line decrease significantly. This includes things like reading with babies or even talking more about emotions and feelings while still at home so kids grow up understanding what these mean.

There is no clear way to avoid the development of ADHD, just as there is no clear way to avoid the development of other mental health disorders either. What you can do, however, is pay close attention to your child's behavior and ask for the help of a specialist if something doesn't seem right.

If a diagnosis is set, the management of the disorder is key in the future development of the child. We will talk more about this in the future chapters of this book.

Chapter 4: Possible Conditions Associated with ADHD

Unfortunately, ADHD is very commonly associated with other medical conditions, both mental and physical. Being aware of these will help you better manage your child if they are diagnosed with ADHD — so we decided to dedicate an in-detail chapter on this topic.

Keep in mind that, if your child has developed ADHD, it does not necessarily mean that they will develop any of the conditions we mention in this chapter. However, it is important for you to be on the lookout and to acknowledge the fact that especially untreated and unmanaged, your child's condition could deviate into other harmful medical issues.

What are these conditions, how are they connected to ADHD, and what are their symptoms?

Read on to find out more.

Anxiety

Anxiety is a mental disorder that is characterized by excessive worry and other symptoms such as insomnia, nausea, excessive sweating, pounding heart-beats, muscle tension, etc.

Symptoms of anxiety include:
- Feeling restless or on edge
- Irritability
- Shortness of breath
- Trembling and twitching muscles
- Dizziness or a feeling of faintness (especially when anxious)
- Headaches
- Sweating
- Feelings of impending doom or danger

There are multiple recognized forms of anxiety, but the most commonly referred to one is Generalized Anxiety Disorder, followed closely by phobias (which sub-categorized according to the trigger that generates the feelings of panic in the patient).

The connection between ADHD and anxiety is not fully understood. However, the way ADHD is typically expressed — by a child being hyperactive and fidgety, and constantly moving about during school, at home, or even in a doctor's office — may downplay the anxiety that accompanies the condition.

Children with ADHD are often more prone to experiencing anxieties as they feel unable to cope with the symptoms of ADHD. This sets them up for a vicious cycle of anxiousness, conflicts with others, and behaviors that intensify these feelings and compound the already difficult conditions that these children face.

Depression

In a clinical sense, depression is a state of serious depression lasting for at least two weeks. It is marked by a diminished, sad, or irritable mood. The person may have thoughts of suicide and past suicidal behavior without consciously remembering these things. Symptoms include (but are not entirely limited to):
- Fatigue or lack of energy
- Loss of interest or pleasure in activities (lethargy)
- Changes in appetite or weight loss/gain
- Sleep difficulties
- Feelings of worthlessness or guilt (low self-esteem)
- Inability to concentrate

- Difficulty remembering details
- Overthinking and overanalyzing situations

Same as in the case of anxiety, the connection between depression and ADHD is not understood at a very detailed level. It is however known that ADHD is very likely to intensify the feelings of depression.

The common symptoms of ADHD can be mistaken for symptoms of depression, and this can make it difficult to identify whether depression is present in a child with ADHD. However, in addition to the common symptoms of ADHD (listed above), children with depression may also experience fatigue or lack of energy; loss of appetite or weight loss; sleep difficulties; feelings of worthlessness or guilt (low self-esteem); difficulty concentrating; and having disconcerting thoughts and feelings that become a common recurrence.

Children (and adults!) who have been diagnosed with ADHD are at a higher risk of developing depressive disorders if left unmanaged.

Learning and Language Disabilities

Learning and language disabilities are defined as conditions characterized by unexpected problems in acquiring one or more of the basic skills. These include reading, writing, spelling, mathematical calculations, and following instructions.

The disability in learning and language can affect any aspect of a child's development. It is not just about academic performance but also includes everyday activities that include interacting with others (both adults and children).

The connection between ADHD and other learning disabilities is not very well understood, but it seems that there is a relationship of causality between an ADHD child's ability to focus and how their learning and language skills develop over time. When these two conditions are present together in a child, they can be very difficult to manage as they interfere with each other's functioning and symptoms.

Gross and Fine Motor Skill Difficulties

Gross and fine motor skill difficulties are characterized by difficulties in the control of large and small muscles, respectively.

Children who have this condition typically have poor coordination, struggle to learn new motor skills, and are thus unable to perform simple everyday tasks that require the use of their hands (such as buttoning a shirt or holding a pencil).

Typically, children develop greater motor control as they progress through childhood. However, children with ADHD typically experience delays in motor development when compared to their peers.

Gross and fine motor difficulties are not as well understood as learning disabilities and language disorders etc. For this reason, the connection between ADHD and these conditions is not as well understood as the connection between ADHD and learning and language disorders.

Obsessive-Compulsive Disorder

Defined as "a type of disorder in which a person has recurrent, intrusive, and distressing thoughts and/or urges that he or she attempts to control with great difficulty," obsessive-compulsive disorder (OCD) is a condition characterized by a preoccupation with some particular activity (such as compulsive hand-washing) (American Psychiatric Association, 2021).

Children who have this condition often experience high anxiety levels when they are around other children. In particular, they may experience extreme anxiety regarding the possibility of losing the attention of others.

The relation between OCD and ADHD is not very well understood, just like in the case of other conditions we tackle in this chapter It is however known that the symptoms associated with OCD can make it difficult for children with ADHD to focus in school and that these two conditions can intensify each other's symptoms.

Oppositional Defiant Disorder

If the conditions mentioned above are more commonly known, Oppositional Defiant Disorder (ODD) is a condition that is not as widely acknowledged these days. This disorder is defined as a pattern of behavior characterized by a lack of compliance with the demands of one's parents or other authority figures (Mayo Clinic, 2021).

Often, Oppositional Defiant Disorder symptoms are more apparent in children with ADHD than they are in other children.

Individuals who have this condition commonly get into trouble with their teachers because they refuse to follow their instructions and can only express themselves with negative comments (or even insults).

It is not necessarily easy to establish a connection between Oppositional Defiant Disorder and ADHD. Sometimes the symptoms of these two disorders overlap leading to uncertainty as to which condition is truly causing the problem.

Obsessive-Compulsive Disorder and Autism Spectrum Disorder are also conditions that are very similar to Oppositional Defiant Disorder in terms of their symptoms.

It is for this reason that it is often difficult to distinguish between these conditions.

Bipolar Disorder

Defined as a condition characterized by extreme changes in mood, bipolar disorder can be difficult to recognize in children but far more commonly acknowledged in adults (Healthline, 2021).

A child with this condition will usually exhibit two opposite behavioral extremes which are manic and depressive episodes.

The manic episodes consist of states of elevated energy levels while the depressive episodes are characterized by periods of low energy levels and feelings of despair.

These two opposite states are quite far from each other and can have a dramatic impact on the lives of those who have bipolar disorder especially when the condition is not managed.

As it was mentioned earlier in the book, children with poorly managed ADHD are more likely to develop Bipolar Disorder, especially as they grow into adulthood.

Tic Disorder

This is a condition characterized by periodic, involuntary motor or verbal tics.

The most common form of this disorder is simple repetitive movements such as blinking, nose tapping, and shoulder shrugging but different people might develop different tics. The pathology of this disorder can be quite difficult to diagnose because it is usually an unpredictable onset of these noises that are not clearly connected to other mental processes.

Tic disorders are almost exclusively diagnosed in children and require the help of a professional to properly manage. Quite often, they are also associated with ADHD because these two conditions are often characterized by hyperactivity and impulsive behaviors (Ratini, 2020).

Tourette Syndrome

Somewhat easy to mistake with the aforementioned condition, Tourette Syndrome is characterized by the use of coarse language, or chronic motor or vocal tics. It is one of the most extreme forms of this disorder as it can lead to other much more severe mental disorders such as OCD or ADHD.

Children with ADHD might also develop Tourette Syndrome though it is much less common.

Also, some people develop Tourette syndrome after having been treated for ADHD. Interestingly, studies show that less than 10% of those diagnosed with ADHD have Tourette Syndrome, but 60 to 80% of those with Tourette develop ADHD. No research points to the treatment of ADHD as being a trigger for the onset of Tourette's, though (CHADD, 2021).

Sleep Disorder

Since in some cases, children with ADHD are characterized as hyperactive, their excessive activity levels can also interfere with their sleep patterns. Along with this, they might have difficulty concentrating at school and performing the tasks required of them during the day thereby decreasing their ability to manage the symptoms of ADHD and its related conditions.

Abuse of Substances

We have already mentioned this earlier in the book but those diagnosed with ADHD are seemingly more likely to develop some sort of substance abuse as adults. The development of addiction can be emotionally taxing on the individual, but it can also further dangerously complicate the ADHD symptoms.

It is very important to note that treatment for ADHD alone might not be enough for addicted individuals and that further, specialized help might be needed.

Other Conditions Associated with ADHD

Research into comorbid conditions is not fully conclusive, so it cannot be said with absolute certainty that there is a direct correlation between them and ADHD. It is also worth noting that many conditions that appear alongside ADHD do not necessarily develop along with ADHD, but some can worsen existing symptoms of ADHD.

Chapter 5: How to Accept Your Child's ADHD Diagnosis

We all hope to bring healthy, happy children into the world who will grow up to have even healthier and happier lives. Unfortunately, genetics as well as a series of other factors sometimes leave their mark on how our children really are. An ADHD diagnosis can leave you, as a parent, feeling like you've done something wrong. It could make you feel helpless and hopeless. And, in the end, it could affect you as much as it does your child.

Before we dive into the sensitivities and details of what it means to be the parent of a child with ADHD, it is important to stop for a moment and learn how to accept this condition. Helping your child better manage the symptoms is tightly connected to how you, as a parent, manage your own reactions to the diagnosis and how you find your balance amidst the turmoil.

As such, we're dedicating Chapter 5 of the book to something that might seem simple but requires continuous hard work on your part as much as it does on your child's: acceptance.

Moving Forward After the Diagnosis

Feeling overwhelmed by sadness, anger, and anxiety once your child has re-ceived an ADHD diagnosis is perfectly normal -- but it is not something you should dwell on for too long. Taking action as soon as possible and learning how to help your child manage their condition as well as how you should man-age your own sensitive situation are both crucial steps you need to take for-ward.

The very first thing to do is learn more about Attention Deficit Hyperactive Disorder. Since you are here reading this book, it is quite clear that you are already on a good path in this respect and that you want to educate yourself more on this topic.

This is a challenging task, so don't feel like your child is the only one who has to work at accepting his or her ADHD diagnosis and its potential conse-quences. As you take in what you've learned about ADHD, and as you begin to understand the many facets of the condition in greater detail, you're also learning more about yourself and how well you manage stress. You are learn-ing about your child's needs too.

Finding the right type of treatment and therapy for your child's specific needs might take time, so don't rush through everything. Try out the different op-tions your medical specialist recommends, and always be prepared to make adjustments. There's no given recipe for the treatment and management of this condition, so you need to manage your expectations.

Do talk to other parents of children with ADHD. This will not only help you find new tactics and techniques you can use in raising your child but will also help you feel less alone in this endeavor. Community has a powerful impact on us, so surrounding yourself with people who really get what you are going through is essential.

How to Manage Emotions as Parents

As mentioned before, you might feel terribly angry at the situation. You obvi-ously want better for your child than having to live with a disorder that will affect their lives well into adulthood.

It is normal to feel frustrated, hurt, and helpless — however, you need to learn how to manage your own emotions in a healthy way.

This can be done by finding support groups and asking for help as soon as you start feeling overwhelmed. If you are feeling depressed or anxious regularly, it would probably do you good to seek professional help. There should be ZERO shame in that. Just like your child, you are going through a lot of adjustments in your life, so it's perfectly normal to ask for help.

And also just like your child, you might have to check in on your own behavior and adapt to the new life lying ahead of you. There IS a lot of hope for the vast majority of children diagnosed with ADHD -- and you really, really have to keep a positive mindset to be able to navigate the bursts of energy, the challenges, and the potential risks you might have to face as the parent of a child with ADHD.

Also, do keep in mind that just because your child has this condition, it doesn't mean you have to completely neglect yourself. Take care of yourself as much as you take care of your child. After all, you're not helping your child if your own mental health is deteriorating. Exercise, eat healthily, and take time to get some fresh air and sunshine. Similarly, as you start to learn about the upsides of your child's condition, don't forget to search for your own positives in all of this.

How to Help Your Child Cope with ADHD

If your child is very young, they might not understand what is going on. They are just happy and energetic, and sometimes they might feel frustrated at how they cannot seem to get it right when it comes to tasks that require a bit of focus. But overall, it is extremely difficult to explain ADHD to a young child, and it shouldn't be your main priority at this time.

But you can start to talk to them about the condition as well as about their emotions, so they feel safe with you and confide in you. The more they know and understand about all of this, the better; however, again, don't expect too much from a child who is only 7 or 8 years old.

The important thing is to explain to them that they have ADHD, but that it is nothing bad: it's just something that makes them happy and energetic, just as some other children's personality is more drawn or introverted, and just as other children have blond hair.

Be honest, be transparent, guide them as you would your other children, and let them know that you are there for them.

We will discuss more the specific techniques you can use when you want to help your child with ADHD, so we will not focus on this for now. However, and this does need emphasis, do keep in mind that your child needs to accept who they are now, rather than grow up feeling that they are different in a negative way. The more positivity you can instill in your child now, the more likely it is that they will grow into an adult who can successfully manage their condition and show the same academic and professional results as everyone else.

Tips to Help Your Family Handle a Child with ADHD

There's no "ADHD parent" textbook or recipe that works for everyone. Every ADHD child is different, every family is different, and every life context is different as well — so you are most likely not going to fit into any kind of "mold."

However, some of the tips you might want to keep in mind as the family supporting and raising a child with ADHD include the following:

- Remember that your child with ADHD isn't lazy. They are just doing what is easier for them. If they seem to be hyperactive, it doesn't mean they don't want to sit still but rather that sitting still is harder for them to do.
- If they seem very impulsive, it means they are more likely to act before thinking things through.
- If they struggle at school, remember that this might be because concentrating is more difficult for them than it is for other children or perhaps the material being presented in class overwhelms them — in which case you should try and see if you can find an alternative educational scenario or a tutor who can come and help out with the academic part of school altogether.
- Make sure your extended family is very well-informed on what ADHD is and how they should behave around your child (and how they can help). Everyone has to be on the same page as to how the child will be raised and helped from hereon, so be sure that they all understand the importance of adults having the right behavior and using the right techniques with your child.
- You are NOT alone in this. Support groups, your extended family, medical providers can all help you navigate the years ahead of you, so that you can, in turn, help your child grow healthily and harmoniously.

Accept that your life will change. Welcoming a child into the world is a change big enough, but learning that they have ADHD can push you into bringing even more structure and even more focus into your life. Your priorities will realign, your house might become a supportive place for raising a child with ADHD, and your own perspective on life might change. But at the end of the day, how you accept all these changes makes all the difference in the world.

Chapter 6: Parenting and Managing A Child with ADHD

Parenting is challenging as it is, but when your child has ADHD, things suddenly become a little more complicated. Do note that we say "a little" and "complicated" in all honesty. Raising a child with ADHD and helping them grow into focused, successful adults is absolutely possible — it's just that you will have to make some adjustments to both your parenting style and your overall lifestyle.

Now, we are not saying it will be a breeze. It won't be. Managing your expectations correctly is of the essence (as we will emphasize in this chapter). But setting yourself up for failure with a negative mindset won't help either.

So, what are some of the most important things to keep in mind when parenting and managing a child with ADHD?

Read on and find out more.

Manage Expectations

We are tackling this first not because it was mentioned above, but because it is the one mindset matter you really have to take care of before you jump into anything else. Managing expectations as the parent of a child with ADHD is crucial because it will help you stay focused and motivated through the years.

First off, don't expect to clear all your child's issues just by reading this chapter (or even this book) and putting things in place. ADHD is a disorder that lasts a lifetime and requires constant work on your part. Your child will need support for their entire life or at least until they become an adult (and even then, they must do regular therapy sessions).

But what about your expectations of the child? What should you be aiming for?

Well, try to set yourself up for success instead of failure. Instead of expecting your child to become the next Nobel Prize winner in their area of interest or expect them to ace all aspects of their life (from school grades to extracurricular activities), try to get them to focus on what they are doing right now and strive for better performance. This stands just as true for children who don't suffer from ADHD, after all.

For example, instead of expecting your child to get an A+ on a particular subject, try focusing on getting them (and yourself) to embrace the challenge and take it head-on. Expect to take it one step at a time, expect it not to be easy, but do expect the best results for the given situation.

Establish a Structure

All children need structure in their lives, but this is especially true in the case of those who have ADHD. Now, we are not here to give you a huge list of things you should do (although we will provide a few actionable resources at the end of this chapter) — instead, we are here to offer you some general tips to help both yourself and your child.

Start by establishing a routine. A routine is something that is repeated over and over again. A schedule helps establish structure in your day (and that extends to your child's day), so try it out as it will help both you as a parent and your child.

Furthermore, establish an environment in your home that is conducive to focus. Some parents have found success in eliminating distractions for example by unplugging the TV and internet connection in their child's room.

Also, try to make sure your child gets a good night's sleep before an important day (like a test day at school). The easier it is for them to focus when they are well-rested, the better their performance (and that goes for all children — not just those who have ADHD).

Finally, you have to consider where your child is placed in school or their extracurricular activities. If you think your child is in an environment that is not best suitable for them, try to make sure they are placed under a more appropriate one. For example, some parents have gotten very good results by moving their ADHD children into smaller classes.

Be Involved

It is important to be involved in your child's activities. Not only will this help them have a better understanding of the challenges they face as a result of ADHD, but it will also help you become more knowledgeable about what your child needs (and how to provide this) at any given time. A good step is to be involved in their various school events and classes — this way, you can see how their day unfolds.

Being involved will help your child know you are there for them no matter what, but it will also help you gain a deeper understanding of what parenting a child with ADHD is like (precisely because you might come in contact with other parents facing a similar situation).

Know How ADHD Affects Your Child

It's easy to look at ADHD as a diagnosis, but it is far more than that. You may never be able to fully understand how your child is feeling, but reading and researching, as well as connecting with other parents in similar situations, will definitely help you better understand how ADHD really affects your child.

Know what your child has to deal with because it will help you better realize the steps you have to take to help them. You need to understand that ADHD is characterized by inattention, hyperactivity, and impulsiveness. While your child might suffer from one or two of these traits more than others, they will still experience all three (at least for a time). This makes it even more important for you to understand what your child has to go through daily.

Focus on Teaching Your Child One Thing at a Time

One of the biggest mistakes some parents make is to try and teach everything at once. They feel like their child's ADHD means that it is essential for them to learn everything at once, but, actually, this will only hurt them. This is especially true when it comes to more complicated things like math and science.

Instead of pushing your child and making them learn so many things at once, try to focus on one thing for a while. The more you bombard your child with

information, the more likely it is that their attention will wane, so always make sure you only "feed" them tidbits of information that are very well-organized and connected to each other.

Talk About It

ADHD is not a common cold; it is a lifelong condition, so it's perfectly normal if you need to talk about it. Ask for specialized help, talk to a friend, and/or discuss matters with your life partner or spouse. Do not hold it inside, as all the negative emotions you are experiencing now might hinder your efforts of helping your child develop harmoniously.

Talk about it with your child too, but do make sure you know how to do it. You don't want to come off as lecturing or patronizing, so ask them questions, be curious, and gently show them what they should do instead. This way, you'll come off as a patient parent rather than someone who feels they have all the answers.

Furthermore, don't make your child feel different. If he or she has an ADHD diagnosis, this will be a constant reminder for the rest of your child's life, which can be frustrating and even hard to deal with. Make your child feel loved and accepted unconditionally and show them you are there to help them manage any challenging situation that might come their way.

Try to Be a Good Example

Being a good example for your child is crucial. You must show good qualities and behavior traits, accept your child's mistakes, and know how to discipline them in the right way.

Follow what you feel you should do rather than chase after what your child's "presumed" behavior should be. You are their parent, and if you set a good example for them, it should start with knowing that neither your child, nor you, are meant to fit in cookie-cutter behaviors.

Remember, children do what they see, not what they are told (and this is true for children who don't have ADHD too!)

Spend Special Time Together Every Day

Always make sure to spend special time with your ADHD child. Otherwise, they're going to start feeling neglected, and they might act up as a response. Talk to them about their day, ask them about their feelings, congratulate them

for their accomplishments, and help them find solutions for their problems. Your child may be young, but they have issues too. Showing them you are there to help will make them trust you more as well as provide them a sense of structure and security (which is incredibly important for a child with ADHD).

Work with Your Child's School

Never let your child get into the habit of ignoring their homework or not turning it in. This will only make things worse for them, and you'll probably end up with a disruptive and unruly child on your hands. Get in touch with their teacher frequently and be as understanding as possible. Many teachers will be able to provide you with strategies to help your child succeed, so it's important not to ignore them when they do offer advice.

Connect with Others for Support and Awareness

As mentioned above, seeking others who are in similar situations can help tremendously. It is one of the most important things you can do for yourself. Being there for others as they go through their own challenges, and offering support yourself, will help you maintain a sense of perspective that I could not have otherwise.

Also, joining online forums or maintaining social media pages and groups is a great way to keep up with what's happening in your community and to stay informed about the latest news about ADHD, treatments, therapy, and techniques other parents use with their children.

Find Out If You Have ADHD

As mentioned earlier in the book, research shows there might be a genetic connection with the development of ADHD. You might even suffer from it as an adult and not be diagnosed (mostly because your symptoms have either worn off or because you haven't been fully aware of them). Running a checkup on yourself will help you determine if you have ADHD and take adequate measures (because remember, your child will want to mimic what you do, not do what you tell them to do).

Learn to Estimate Time Better

This is a general life skill, of course, but it becomes even more important when you are parenting a child with ADHD. The better you know how to estimate time, the more structure you will be able to add to your child's life. Estimating time better will help you manage the tasks you have to do better, organize your child's day better, and ensure that their schedule is being kept.

Furthermore, better time management will help you account for potential delays in how your child accomplishes a task. Remember that it is very difficult for them to focus and that they are not doing this intentionally or just because they are throwing a tantrum -- so being the mature, well-prepared one will help both you and your child manage any challenge that may appear in your daily schedule.

Other Tips

Other bits of advice you might want to keep in mind as the parent of a child who has ADHD include the following:

- Remember that this is a disorder. Yes, you might get frustrated sometimes and you might end up downright angry. But don't lose your temper and certainly don't yell — these things are not only counterproductive to your efforts, but they might actually do more harm than good (and that goes for your child too).
- Don't bottle up your emotions. As mentioned above, you should have a support system and you should talk about what you are feeling. Being a good parent is all about being balanced -- and bottling up your emotions will eventually lead to the exact opposite of that.
- Compromise. You might not "win" every day, and you might sometimes have to accept small mistakes and make compromises. That's OK, the journey to successfully managing ADHD is not easy and it most definitely isn't a straight line.
- Believe in your child. It might not seem like it now, but your child is going to do great. They will succeed, they will grow up to be healthy and balanced, and they will be happy. They need your help now (like every child needs), but with that help, they will achieve what they never thought was possible.
- Know you have support. There are plenty of support and parenting groups out there, so make sure you take advantage of them even if you don't use them right away.
- Take breaks. You cannot and should never, ever run yourself out of batteries. Allow your child to take breaks as well, and always make sure you are well-rested, relaxed, and energized. Yes, you are working

hard to help your child live a better life, but that doesn't mean you can allow yourself to go non-stop, without a single break. Allow family, friends, or a babysitter to spend some time with your child now and again; it can do wonders for your mental health and energy levels.

- Practice self-care. This is in the same line of thought as what we mentioned above: if you don't take care of yourself, you won't be able to care for your child. It's as simple as that. Take time every day to do something you enjoy and relax. It might be a quick session of meditation or working out in the morning or a late-night bath -- whatever it is, make sure you allow yourself to relax.
- Take care of your physical health too. Move as much as possible, eat healthily, drink water, reduce the amount of caffeine you pour into your body, and, generally, try to be mindful of everything that happens to you, physically. Your child needs a strong parent, not someone who is not taking care of their own health!
- Make sure your child eats healthy too. Your child needs good energy and nutrients in their bodies, not junk, so always keep them away from things that might spike up their negative behaviors (such as sugar or caffeine, for example). Stock your house with healthy snacks and foods, and make sure you eat the same things as well.
- Make sure your child's schedule is as simple as possible. Don't make your child's life complicated, but also don't get in the habit of "doing twice as much" because you feel like you have to. Stick to a schedule that allows your child to focus deeply and accomplish one thing at a time, and use timeouts if needed.
- Create a quiet and safe space for your child to learn. Everybody's environment is different, and some children do better in a noisy classroom setting, while others thrive in a more tranquil setting. Because your child has ADHD, they will need a very peaceful setting for their educational activities, as this will lower the odds that they get distracted.
- Don't be afraid to use clocks and timers. This will help your child gain a sense of routine and structure with every task they run. For instance, if you always tell them that brushing their teeth should take an X amount of minutes, they will be more likely to focus on the task at hand.
- Encourage your child to move as much as possible. Physical exercise will be good for their mind and their bodies, and it will help them focus better and sleep better as well.
- Make sure sleep time is respected and that it follows a routine. For instance, you might need some buffer time between "active time" and

"sleep time," as this will help your child cool down and prepare for a night of restful sleep.

- Establish clear, immediate rewards for tasks done well. It could be praises, privileges, or activities your child enjoys, for example. Also, try to change rewards frequently, to keep your child's interest high.
- Establish consequences for negative behaviors too, and spell them out to your child. These consequences should be immediate, and they can be things like removing privileges or setting up time-outs.
- Help your child make friends. Being social is incredibly important for human beings, and your child is no exception to the rule. Speak candidly to your child about making friends and the challenges they might have to face, and teach them how to handle these challenges. Play role-based games with your child to help them understand how they might feel (and how to react in different social situations). Also, be careful with the playmates you select for your child and only invite one or two of them at a time (as more of them might trigger negative behaviors in your child).

Yes, being the parent of a child with ADHD requires continuous work, and it can be challenging even if you are the most patient person in the world. However, the more work you put into your methods now, the more they will pay off when you see your child behaving well and growing up to be happy, healthy, and successful in their area of interest.

Chapter 7: Looking at the Bright Side of Being the Parent of an ADHD Child

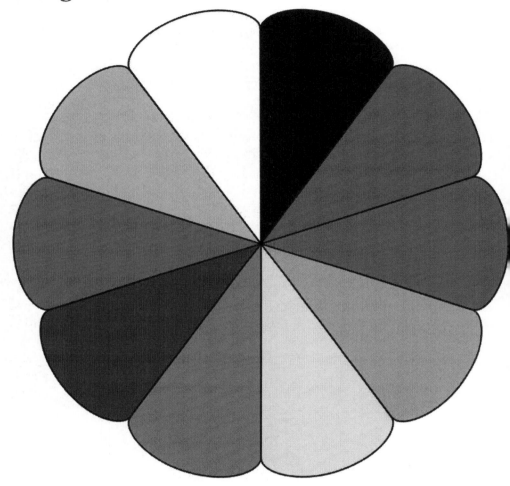

As we were discussing earlier in the book, it is extremely important to maintain a positive mindset when you are the parent of an ADHD child. It might not always be easy given that you are truly facing a challenging situation. However, looking at the bright side of parenting an ADHD child can definitely help you maintain your positivity and, overall, your balance.

Here are some of the good parts of being the parent of a child with ADHD.

The Energy: SO Much Energy!

Let's face it, having an ADHD child can be fun! As a parent of an ADHD child, you will most likely find yourself smiling and laughing more than usual. Imagine what people say when they see how much energy your child has!

Imagine your child running around smiling and laughing their way through the house. Imagine them not able to sit still for five minutes or more because they are always on the move. Imagine them constantly talking non-stop and acting as if he has been placed in a completely different state of mind.

Those are not inherently bad traits. They are, in fact, the characteristics of a happy, healthy child. Yes, you do have to help your child manage these things and bring balance into their lives, but looking at them happily bouncing around without a single worry in the world can give you a special sense of satisfaction (same as it would for any parent, really).

The Spontaneity

ADHD children are very spontaneous, so you can bet your money you won't get bored very easily with this explosion of energy around the house. That's actually good news because it will help you find real joy in every single day of your life.

Sometimes, your child's spontaneity might get them into trouble. But most times it could just be little things like the way they are amazed by how flowers grow or them doing something really special to show you their love.

On many days, being the parent of an ADHD child can feel like constantly trying to turn off a ticking bomb. But then there are also so many days when it feels like you're living next to an explosion of color, joy, and genuine human beauty that somehow it all balances out!

Being Creative and Inventive

A child with ADHD is naturally creative and inventive. Their mind buzzes with ideas and they are always looking for new ways to try new things. They are especially likely to be creative when it comes to their artwork or stories. In fact, there is a good chance that one or more of their activities may possibly be an attempt to write a book, play a musical instrument, learn how to cook or sing, etc.

This can be a blessing and a curse for the parent to know about because you will most likely find yourself stuck with the constant care of their needs and demands. However, when focusing on the positives, you will see that your child could make an amazing artist one day — we're more than sure that this will only help you stay motivated to help them as much as you can.

Being Hyper-Focused

Not many people realize this but sometimes ADHD children can be hyper-focused on one thing or task. Sometimes this may seem like it is a problem but it isn't. Many ADHD children have at least one focused trait that they just can't help.

And these traits don't always have to be negative. There are some fantastic examples of great focus abilities in both artists and athletes, stories that go to show that being hyper-focused can get you pretty far in life. This is actually a trait many people wish they had or cultivate on their own. You can celebrate the fact that your child is naturally inclined to stay very focused on something they enjoy doing or are interested in.

What Research Says About the Benefits of ADHD

The situation might look complicated and downright scary right now, but research shows there are actual benefits to ADHD. Managed correctly, your child's behavior can actually improve over time and they can learn how to deal with their symptoms quite successfully.

Moreover, according to studies, people with ADHD seem to perform better in creative tasks, both as adults and as children (Healthline, 2021). It is perhaps no surprise that so many celebrities, athletes, and business people are open about their ADHD diagnoses and even admit that it has helped them perform better. Some examples include Adam Levine (musician), Channing Tatum (actor), Karina Smirnoff (ballet dancer), Scott Kelly (US senator and astronaut), Simone Biles (gymnast), and Lisa Ling (journalist).

An ADHD diagnosis does not have to feel like the end of the world. Instead, allowing yourself to focus on the positives will help you as a parent and your child as well, precisely because it will help you keep your mind off of everything that could go wrong (and onto those things that could go exceptionally well).

Stay positive! You are at the beginning of a long journey filled with ups and downs and that's scary. But then again, show us a parent who wasn't scared about what lies ahead of them -- we bet you can't!

Chapter 8: Treatments for ADHD

Although it is not entirely understood, ADHD is now a lot better treated and managed than in the past. As you dig deeper in your research on this condition and how you can help your child develop harmoniously, you will also learn that there are a lot of treatment options available.

In this chapter, we will discuss some of the more common ones and explain what exactly they entail — read on if you want to find out more.

Stimulant and Non-Stimulant Medication

Medication may be prescribed to children with ADHD, depending on their specific symptoms and situations. Not only are these types of medications quite widely available, but there are multiple sub-categories you should be aware of as well:

Central Nervous System Stimulants

These medications help maintain focus and attention and may have the side effect of improving mood. Stimulant medications aren't used in children under the age of six years old having been associated with more serious health risks including heart problems.

Non-Stimulant Medication

Behavioral therapy is the most commonly used non-stimulant treatment for ADHD. It's often a form of counseling or therapy that focuses on the child's behavior patterns rather than their symptoms.

Aside from behavioral therapy, however, you might also find a medication that does not stimulate the central nervous system. At the moment, atomoxetine is the only non-stimulant medication approved by the FDA, but do consult with your doctor to find out more about options in the same variety of medications (Robinson et al, 2020).

Side Effects of Medication

Like all types of medication, both stimulant and non-stimulant treatments for ADHD can have side effects. In the case of stimulant medication for ADHD, the side effects could include (Silver, 2019):

- Weight loss (due to decreased appetite)
- Dry mouth (difficulties lubricating your mouth and swallowing)
- Sleep issues (trouble sleeping, insomnia, or nightmares)
- Decreased appetite

There is also some evidence that stimulant medication can occasionally cause tics in children.

Non-stimulant medication can also show side effects, including the following (Bhandari, 2019):

- Sudden weight gain
- Weight loss
- Dry mouth
- Increased appetite
- Anxiety (especially in children who have not responded well to non-stimulant medication)

Not all children are alike and that stands just as true for ADHD children too. Your child may or may not show side effects (just as they may or may not be prescribed medication for their condition). Only a medical professional can

help you decide on the next steps forward when it comes to whether or not your child should start or continue to take medical treatments for their ADHD.

Therapeutic ADHD Treatments

In addition to medication, therapy can also help ADHD children manage their symptoms and behaviors. Some of the most efficient types of therapy applied in the case of ADHD include the following:

Psychotherapy

Therapy includes counseling sessions, psychotherapy, and behavior therapy sessions (in which children learn coping mechanisms in place of their behaviors).

Behavioral Therapy

This form of therapy focuses on changing inappropriate behavior patterns. It aims at helping children stop relapsing into old habits and recognizing the triggers that lead them to their old ways. Behavioral therapy is also commonly used in conjunction with medication and/or school-based interventions.

Social Skills Training

Based on the premise that social skills are a critical aspect of one's ability to cope with ADHD, this type of therapy helps teach children coping strategies and new ways of interacting with others.

Family Therapy

This form of therapy focuses on helping the child and their family members achieve better communication and coping mechanisms for dealing with different situations.

Support Groups

Support groups are also a highly efficient tool when it comes to helping children with ADHD. This is especially true for families with ADHD children that have a hard time coping with their child's symptoms and behaviors.

Parenting Skills Training

This type of therapy is designed to help parents better support their child's success in school and at home through goal setting and implementation. It also includes a focus on helping them recognize triggers that lead to poor behavior.

Behavioral Interventions for Home and School

Because ADHD has been proven to negatively affect academic performance, students must receive appropriate treatment to overcome the challenges they're facing. This form is a series of educational and behavioral interventions applied by teachers, supporting staff, or specialized education personnel.

Although this is not an all-inclusive list (as we will discuss the matter later on in the book), these are some of the absolute basic interventions for home and school which are known to help children with ADHD:

- Build a schedule. Parents should keep track of their child's daily activities and provide them with a schedule. This helps children better plan and organize their day.
- Organize everyday items. Color coding and organizing all their stuff can help children with ADHD achieve better focus and attention.
- Use homework and notebook organizers. This is especially helpful for children with ADHD who have a hard time finishing their work on time.
- Ask about using a computer in class. Although not an actual intervention, asking the school if your child can use a computer in class might help them stay more organized and focused. However, it is worth noting that the results of doing this may vary from one case to another.
- Use positive reinforcement. This is especially true when it comes to dealing with ADHD children. Parents must understand that keeping their mood light and giving them some positive feedback whenever they do something right can help reinforce positive behavior.
- Talk with your doctor. When it comes to dealing with ADHD home and school interventions, it's also important to speak with a medical professional. They will be able to help you make the necessary adjustments for your child's home and school-based issues.

Yes, there are a lot of ways you can help your child, and this has been just brushing the surface on the main methods available out there. Your doctor and therapist will definitely help you find the best solutions for your specific case!

Chapter 9: ADHD Behavior Therapy for Children

As mentioned in the previous chapter, behavioral therapy is one of the most widespread treatments used in the case of children with ADHD. In this chapter, we will talk a little more about what it actually is, what you should expect, and why this type of therapy tends to be so common in the treatment of this disorder.

So, without further ado, let's dive in!

What Is Behavior Therapy for Children with ADHD

The basics of this type of therapy for children with ADHD are based on the concept of replacing negative behaviors with positive ones. This is done by working on the child's deficiencies and problem behaviors. According to the psychologist who developed this method, it relies much more on teaching rather than behavior modification per se, which is how this therapy is often labeled in some literature (Cram, 2020).

Of course, there's a fine line between the two meanings, but it might be worth keeping in mind because it will help you shift your focus from "behavior changes" to "learning process" (which is actually more similar to what behavioral therapy will bring into your lives).

In short, this treatment method is based on specific changes that can be made when it comes to the child's behaviors. One of these changes can consist of replacing a negative behavior with a positive one or simply reducing the frequency of the problem behavior so that it does not occur as often.

In addition to this, there are other aspects to this type of therapy for children with ADHD. For instance, you can find other aspects such as helping your child to be more self-confident or to perform better socially.

How Exactly Is Behavioral Therapy Helpful for Children with ADHD?

Behavioral therapy for children with ADHD is based on specific aspects of the child's behaviors. However, this treatment does not simply deal with negative or problem behaviors. It also focuses on reinforcing positive behaviors that can help improve your child's performance in school, limit his or her problems, and help him or her to be a happier person as well.

In the case of behavioral therapy for children with ADHD, you will meet with your psychologist or therapist who will help you understand what parts of your child's behaviors can be modified and changed. Then he or she will explain to you how these changes are supposed to happen and teach you how to perform them properly and safely.

How ADHD Behavioral Therapy Teaches Focus

Behavior therapy doesn't magically bring focus into anyone's life. Instead, it allows us to "reprogram" our thinking to bring it about. One of the methods used to do this is called "thought stopping."

In a nutshell, whenever your child is feeling distracted, he or she can look away from whatever they're looking at. When they do this, it will help them to redirect their focus onto something else that can be useful and productive for them.

Another technique used during this therapy is the act of replacing distractive thoughts with positive ones. This way, your child will feel more focused and can be more productive.

ADHD Behavioral Therapy Goals That Work

ADHD behavioral therapy is most effective when you (and your child's therapist) establish clear goals for the entire process. Some of the ADHD behavioral therapy goals that are used include the following:

1. Making your child feel more confident in himself or herself.

2. Reducing negative behaviors so that they do not occur as often.

3. Helping your child improve his or her social skills and relationships.

4. Helping your child to complete schoolwork properly and on time especially if he or she has problems with maintaining focus on tasks while at home.

5. Helping your child to learn how to cope with stress and anxiety especially when it comes to situations that may be difficult or stressful for him or her.

While this may not sound like a lot of goals, they have been very effective for children with ADHD, and many parents have found that these goals can help them enjoy their lives more than they did before.

What Makes a Good ADHD Behavioral Therapy Plan

Every child is different, and thus, every child will require a different ADHD behavioral therapy plan. However, there are some general guidelines that your therapist can follow to help you come up with a plan that will be more suitable for your child and his or her needs. Some of these guidelines include:

- Evidence-based strategies. If there's a certain method or technique that has been proven to be effective, then it should be considered during the treatment process.
- Short-term objectives and goals. As you can imagine, what you're aiming for isn't something that can be achieved overnight, so your therapist or psychologist will need to establish short-term goals for you to reach during the duration of this therapy.

- Long-term objectives and goals. This is not a one-time process but a continuous one you, your child, and your therapist will keep on working on. ADHD cannot be actually "cured" but it can be successfully managed and continuously working on long-term objectives and goals helps with this.

How to Launch Your ADHD Behavioral Therapy Plan

When your child starts with their behavioral therapy plan, you want to make sure that they are ready and that the entire process will not be too confusing for them. To do this, you will need to:

1. Explain to them what ADHD behavioral therapy is all about as well as how it works.

2. Make sure they understand that this treatment isn't a punishment or a way of reprimanding them for certain behaviors but simply a means of helping them to improve the way they approach tasks and challenges.

3. Talk to your child about the objectives and goals you and your child's therapist have set for ADHD behavioral therapy.

4. Talk to them about the changes they are going to experience since their therapy is supposed to make them more focused, confident, and happy.

5. Spend time with them so that they can become comfortable with everything that's going on in their life right now, including this treatment. After all, being uncomfortable may make them distracted and not as open to learning new things.

ADHD Guide to Behavior Therapy

Of course, we couldn't include everything there is to know about behavior therapy in just one short segment (there are entire libraries written about this). However, if we had to narrow it all down to just a handful of guidelines, they would be the following:

- Make sure your child is fully aware (and understands) the rules. If you want your child to behave properly, then he or she needs to know what behaviors are considered appropriate and which ones aren't.
- Give clear commands. This is very important, as you want to make sure that your child understands what you're doing and what he or she needs to do for you to improve his or her behavior. If they break the rules, simply state what they have done so.

- Don't expect perfection. It's only natural to expect your child to do everything right, but that's just not going to happen in the real world. However, you can create a positive learning environment so that they can improve their behavior and get used to the idea of having rules and being responsible.

- Create a system for rewards and consequences (such as a point/token system, for example). This is a very common and effective technique when it comes to behavior therapy. If your child is doing something that he or she should be doing, then he or she gets a point for listening to you. If, on the other hand, they don't do what you ask of them, you have to establish clear consequences they are very aware of (and enforce them as well).

- Adjust your discipline techniques according to your child's age. If your child is still a little too young to understand the consequences, then you may want to use alternatives such as watching TV with him or her and listening to music to distract them.

- Talk to your child's teachers and ask them if they could use a similar behavioral system. This will not only help your child to follow the rules, but it will also remind him or her of the consequences of their actions.

- Make sure the entire family knows what you are doing (and actively supports you in this). All of your family members should be involved in the decisions you make for your child, and they should all agree on what is appropriate.

Of course, this is not all there is to know about behavioral therapy but the basics you should be aware of before you take on this journey. With patience, the right techniques, and adequate additional treatments, your child will definitely be better at managing their negative patterns!

Chapter 10: Life Skills Your Child Needs to Master

Studies show that ADHD persists in adolescence in 50 to 80% of the cases, and in adulthood in 35-65% of the cases (CHADD, 2021). Those might look like very high numbers, but the reality is that the right treatments and management systems can lower the odds that your child ends up having severe issues well into their teenage and adult years.

In essence, together with your child and your child's therapist, you should focus on helping the little one develop essential life skills that will help them perform better. Every parent needs to do this with their child, regardless of whether or not they have ADHD. However, in the case of ADHD children, the symptoms might make it a little more challenging (but definitely not impossible!).

Here are some life skills your ADHD child will have to master:

Independence

All children need to be taught how to do things independently and, over time, to become self-sufficient. Let me illustrate this with an example:

If a child likes playing video games and you allow them to play for hours on end, then they won't learn how to make their own meals, do their own laundry,

plan their own social schedules, etc. They will simply remain dependent on you for every little thing!

So if your ADHD child is having trouble listening or following simple instructions at home (e.g. doing the dishes, taking out the garbage, doing homework, etc.), then it would be a good idea to sit down with them and teach them how to do these simple tasks.

Social Skills

ADHD children tend to experience difficulties when it comes to social skills. This might be because of the way they look at things or they might simply not know how to talk properly. With the right approach and treatments, however, children with ADHD can learn how to properly socialize, make friends, and grow relationships with other people.

Time Management

Most children with ADHD have a hard time with it but the key is to teach them that they have to make a schedule and stick to it. They will need their own planner or diary for this to be possible, as well as different tools to make effective use of it. It is not at all impossible for a child with ADHD to develop very good time management skills, especially if they are taught how to organize their time from a very young age.

Organization

Another thing that ADHD children struggle with within their lives is organization. There are times when a child will be able to engage in both hyperactive and impulsive behavior and other times when they will be quite calm and organized. Therefore, it would be a good idea for parents to teach their children about the value of the organization as early as possible.

This way, the child will know what it means to have a well-ordered life and will also learn how to keep everything neat and tidy, both in their physical surroundings, and when it comes to how they organize their thoughts.

Money Management

Many people with ADHD are great at getting into trouble when it comes to money, lying, stealing, or any other type of crime that involves money. An

ADHD child will need to learn how to control their impulses and focus on achieving realistic goals. For this to happen, parents should teach their children about budgeting, planning, and saving money.

Taking Medications

A large number of children with ADHD actually do very well with medication. However, this is not an easy road to navigate since they can develop side effects and require adjustments in the dosage as they grow older. Therefore, your child must take his or her medications regularly and appropriately (and that they learn the importance of doing so).

Relationships

Some adult cases of ADHD actually maintain the same behavior as they did when they were children. Whether that is a good thing or a bad thing depends on the person. However, it does make sense to teach them how to build and maintain relationships with other people.

For them to build and maintain relationships, children with ADHD should learn how to pay attention in class, develop friendships, and organize their day around meeting other people in social situations.

Anger Management

Children with ADHD tend to be very emotional and angry, so it is important for you as a parent to teach them how to handle these emotions and how to make sure they do not affect them (or others around them).

Wise Decision-Making

Though ADHD children might be very impulsive and quick to react, they do not necessarily make the best decisions, to begin with. They can learn how to make better decisions by learning from their mistakes and watching others who are successful in similar situations.

The more they learn about the consequences of their actions the more likely it is that they will make better decisions in the future.

As mentioned before, an ADHD diagnosis does not have to mean your child cannot grow into a successful, functional, and independent adult. It takes time

to get there, and it definitely takes effort on all ends. It is more than doable, especially with the knowledge we now have of this disorder.

Chapter 11: Managing a Child with ADHD Away from Home

Managing a child with ADHD at home is one thing. You have structures, a safe space, and everything set up to help your child focus and accomplish tasks. However, you cannot spend all your life at home and neither can your child. Making sure your child is on their best behavior away from home can be a challenge, but it can be even more difficult when you're away from home with them.

It's not impossible, though. Here are some tips you might want to keep in mind.

In the Car

You'll need to plan what your children will be allowed to do in the car. When you're away from home with them, they'll be able to do whatever they want. However, you'll want a system that helps them focus and pay attention as long

as possible. A good way to implement this is by rewarding your children for doing something good in the car. It can be as simple as giving them five minutes to play a game they enjoy or letting them sing along to their favorite tunes.

When you're not in the car, you'll want to make sure you have a plan. If they're old enough to understand, you can ask them what the rules are and why it is important that they follow those rules.

It's also important that you keep all of their things packed easily and ready to go. There's no time for digging through suitcases or backpacks when you're trying to get on the road as quickly as possible.

Make sure you have their distractions ready to go too. If they can play a game or listen to music in the car, have it ready to go before you leave the house.

In the Store

When you're at the store, have a list of things you need, and stick to the list. Shopping can seem like a big chore for a child with ADHD, so make sure you have a plan in place.

It's also important to understand that not everything needs to be purchased right away. Sometimes it makes more sense to wait until later, and sometimes it just doesn't make sense. Whatever you do, make sure you stick to the list. If you run out of something, don't panic. If it's possible, go back to the store later and grab what you need. Or, if it's not possible, just buy something else instead. The idea here is that you shouldn't go in circles looking for a specific item as your child will find it easier to get distracted and even throw a tantrum.

When it comes to stores and shopping centers, it is a good idea to keep an eye on your child's behavior. Your child might just want to grab a toy or take something off the shelf without paying for it. Sometimes they might get a little loud but that's okay. What is important is to keep an eye out and to stop them if they are doing anything that is not on your list.

Public Misbehavior

Another thing you'll want to keep in mind when you're away from home is that children with ADHD tend to misbehave more outside of the house. It could be in the store, on a playdate, or at school. When you are away from home, it can seem like the ADHD behaviors are out of control.

Don't worry, though! You don't have to let your child get away with all of these behaviors. Be proactive and give them consequences. When they misbehave, take something away from them. It could be as simple as taking away a toy for

five minutes or it could be something bigger such as taking away their video game time. The idea is that you want to let your child know what the consequences are for their behaviors and that those consequences are important to you.

Do your best to manage a child with ADHD when they are away from home by planning ahead and rewarding good behavior too. You can give them five extra minutes on their favorite game or anything else you know they enjoy doing.

Do not make a scene out of showing your child they did something wrong. Even if you feel upset on the inside about it, you should never show that to your kid. You must always show them respect and love no matter what they do.

Peer Relationships

As mentioned before, ADHD children might sometimes have a hard time developing healthy relationships and that includes with their peers as well. As a parent, you will want to help your child shape healthy relationships with people their age. Make sure you give them lots of opportunities for positive attention from their peers. They might not receive enough of that in school so make sure to provide it when you can. Also, remember they should always know how proud you are of them for taking up sports or music. There's nothing like seeing your child excel and hold a trophy at the end of the season!

You might also want to help your child find new friends. They will always need people around their age to talk to and play with. Don't hesitate to put them in a new school if you think they'd be happiest in that new environment. It might not be the easiest thing for them, but it will be better for them in the long run.

If your child has a hard time making friends, it could mean that they are having trouble fitting into a group of children. This is common, especially among children that suffer from ADHD. However, it doesn't have to be a life-long condition. With help, care, and attention, your child can and will make friends.

Other Situations Outside of Home

In addition to what we mentioned above, you might come across different situations outside of your home when you want to know how to manage your child's behavior. Here are some of the essential tips to keep in mind in these situations:

- Keep an eye out for them to make sure they do not get out of line.
- Reward good behaviors and show them that being nice comes with benefits.

- When you're at the park, give them something to throw if they are anxious. You can reward them for being good.
- Remember that it is okay to say no to them and refuse to take them somewhere if they don't behave properly.

Teaching your child how to behave in the presence of other people is a hard thing to do, but it's crucial for further growth and development. After all, you want them to reach a point where they know how to behave nicely on their own without your constant watchful eye guiding them through the perils and anxiety-driving situations of the "real world." Teaching your ADHD child how to be independent is crucial and this is why everything you do now matters so much.

Chapter 12: Improving Social Skills of Children with ADHD

As mentioned before in the book, children with ADHD tend to have a pretty hard time developing social skills. It might not happen to all children with ADHD, but it tends to be a common symptom.

In this chapter, we'll talk about the basic tips you should keep in mind to help your child improve their social skills from a young age.

Provide Immediate, Frequent Feedback

Just like every other skill, social skills need to be practiced for them to be properly developed.

It's important to constantly provide feedback about social skills. This is something that can help you a lot if you have an ADHD child who needs help with their social skills.

If you allow your child to develop it on their own, this will take a lot longer than if you apply some basic techniques and then continue to provide

immediate feedback. Remember that it's important to provide feedback as soon as possible. Don't wait for the next day to talk to your child. Talk to your child immediately after your situation happens so that it'll be fresh in their mind. It's also very important to realize that you're not just criticizing your child or telling them what they did wrong, but rather you're helping them learn what they can do better.

Focus on a Few Areas That Your Child Is Struggling In

A lot of people tend to get so overwhelmed that they try to fix every single thing about their child that they see as a problem.

You can improve social skills with your child by focusing on a few areas where your child might be struggling rather than trying to teach every single social skill that your child should have.

For example, you could focus on the following areas:

1. Reading Social Situations – With younger children, reading facial expressions is one of the best things you can do for them.
2. Understanding Body Language – Many kids, especially kids with ADHD, get confused about body language.
3. Following Directions – This is a skill that has many different faces and can be difficult to improve by just showing your child how to do them.
4. Managing Multiple Activities at Once – This is a big issue for a lot of children with ADHD because they have trouble switching their attention from one task to another.
5. Listening to Instructions – Children with ADHD often tend to be very independent and might not want to listen to instructions.
6. Avoiding Negative Conversations – This is something that a lot of ADHD children have a hard time understanding and, as a parent, you can help them avoid negative conversations (as well as understand why doing this is important).
7. Avoid Asking Open-Ended Questions – Sometimes, this is something people tend to do around ADHD children and they don't really realize how it can be hurtful for them. An open-ended question can de-focus the child and make it more difficult for them to find an answer, so it should be avoided (as much as possible, of course).
8. Not Interrupting – This is something you can help your child learn from an early age so that they'll manage their time better in the future. When they avoid interrupting, they can focus on the essential information that's being communicated.

9. Talking About Feelings – If your child struggles with talking about feelings, this can also be improved later on to get them to understand how other people feel.

By focusing on one or two of these social skills at a time you allow yourself and your child to take things slowly and truly let the lessons sink in (before they become habits).

Schedule Playdates with Only One or Two Friends at a Time

One of the most common social skills improvement tips is to avoid playing with more than two other children at a time. This can be very difficult for those with ADHD because they often tend to get distracted and lose focus very easily when they're around too many people at one time.

It's also very important that the children you play with have different interests. This will help your child understand that not everyone's the same and will help them understand and learn from others in different ways.

To avoid having too many people at a time play with your child, don't schedule playdates for the entire group to go to one place all at once. Instead, have your child invite two friends over and then get in touch with the child's parents to see if it would be OK for them to come along too.

Increase Your Child's Social Awareness

Becoming more aware of your child's social skills is an important step in improving their social skills. This doesn't mean you need to tell or show your child what they did wrong every single time. It means sitting down with them and letting them know how they can improve their social skills.

For example, if your child is very shy when talking to new people, let them know that they can start by introducing themselves to the person. Furthermore, do not assume that your child knows how to start a conversation with someone new. Talk to them about why they might be shy or even fearful and address issues one by one.

Create Opportunities for Friendship Development

Making sure your child gets plenty of opportunities to develop their friendships is one of the best social skills improvement tips. Some of these opportunities include:

1. Group sports – This is a great way to see how your child reacts and interacts with others, especially when competing.

2. After school activities – Once school lets out, children tend to avoid spending time together because they have a lot going on (and forget about the fact that they're supposed to be improving their social skills).

3. Host a party – You can have a sleepover at your house and invite a couple of children who your child enjoys being around.

4. Field trip – Take your child on field trips that will allow them to interact with other children like going to the zoo or going to watch their favorite team play.

Work with the School to Improve Peer Status

If your child's social skills are suffering at school, take some time to work with the teacher to help get them on the right track.

If your child is struggling because of the way they're being treated at school, especially if their peers make fun of their behaviors, tell them how you're going to handle it.

Last, but not least, make sure they understand that you will stand up for them and talk to the teacher if necessary.

Teach Skills Directly and...Practice, Practice, Practice!

Social skills are not something that you just read and move on to the next topic. It's something that needs to be practiced over and over again until your child can use these skills in their own life. You cannot expect things to happen overnight or after one discussion. Expect the change to come slowly, in time, so arm yourself with patience and help your child practice their social skills as often as possible.

Like with most of the skills ADHD children have to learn, getting social won't be easy. But it will be so worth it!

Chapter 13: ADHD at School

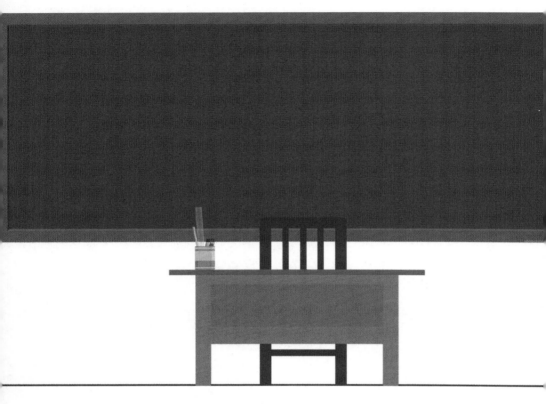

While you might not be able to spend time with your child at school, you can work with them and their teachers to make sure they succeed. As we said before, seeing your child succeed at school is not at all impossible, especially if some basic tips are kept in mind.

Here they are:

Setting Up Your Child for School Success

When you set up for school success, you'll be looking for several things. As a parent, your top priority should always be making sure your child is physically and mentally ready to go to school. If you've not already done so, it's probably a good idea to have a physical checkup at the doctor before school starts.

Furthermore, you also want to discuss with your child some of the biggest challenges that they're likely to face at school and work with them on strategies for handling some of these difficulties ahead of time. You might find that some of the signs or symptoms your child experiences while at school can be better controlled with a little bit of preparation.

The most common issues you might want to prepare your child for are:

1. Seat locations Depending upon where your child sits in class, they may have more or less difficulty paying attention and staying engaged in classwork.

2. Peer pressure

3. Changing class schedules

4. Locker assignment and storage areas

5. Being the new kid in class

6. Learning a new school calendar

7. Sorting through student files and paperwork (to avoid being overwhelmed)

8. Getting used to feeling like a prisoner in their own classroom (If they've not been worried about this already)

9. Having to make up work that they missed in class

10. Adjusting to a new school schedule (changing recess periods, etc.)

11. Classroom discipline and how students are treated by teachers (Does it seem like teachers treat them differently than other kids?)

12. Safety concerns (Is there a lot of violence or bullying in the neighborhood? Are there any threats of violence against individual students?)

13. Kids feel like they can't talk to adults when they want to discuss something while at school.

How Can Teachers Help Kids with ADHD?

Both parents and teachers should see each other as allies when it comes to ensuring the success of a child with ADHD. Some of the things teachers can do to help kids with ADHD include the following:

1. Avoid negative comments and attitudes

2. Address concerns in private or with the whole class, not one child

3. Use concrete examples to illustrate points of learning (For example, say "Pick up the math textbook" instead of "Let's do math") Your child is far more likely to listen if you give them something specific to do to follow along with what you're asking them to do.

4. Listen to the child's concerns and complaints and address them fairly

5. Use positive reinforcement whenever possible

6. Keep students' attention during group discussions by making sure everyone is on task

7. Make rules fair for everyone and make sure they see the point of rules and policies especially when it comes to disciplinary issues

8. Realize that kids with ADHD are more likely to blurt out or say things they shouldn't have said so don't make a big deal about it

9. Avoid arguing disputes with students, as this could de-focus a child with ADHD and make them feel confused.

10. Don't become impatient if your student fidgets in class. Remember that they do not want to be this way and that your goal is to help them stay focused.

11. Avoid talking too much, especially in front of the child when you know they can't keep up. This is almost impossible, so don't beat yourself up over this one. Have an action plan and stick to it.

Tips for Working with the Teachers

You should collaborate with your child's teachers. Here are some things to know about doing this:

1. If you're going to see a teacher about an issue between the two of you, try to make your child an ally in the discussion.

2. Share your child's strengths and weaknesses with the teacher so they can work together to help them improve at school.

3. Make sure you understand what has already been done for and with your child before you enter into these discussions with teachers.

4. If you know of possible issues or concerns to discuss with your child, say so before you enter into the discussion with the teacher.

5. If your child is having difficulty managing their emotions or not feeling comfortable in class, talk about it with them before you see the teacher.

6. Schedule visits to see teachers in advance of implementing change. Make sure they understand why it's important to take some time to work things out ahead of time.

7. Get ready for constructive criticism.

Developing and Using a Behavior Plan

As discussed earlier in the book, behavioral psychology shows great results when it comes to children with ADHD. If your child is having trouble with a

particular behavior, he or she will appreciate any behavioral plan that you implement. Here are some things that your child's teachers and school counselor might suggest:

1. Create a reward chart that has creative rewards for ideas like passing their science test, doing their homework in class, doing extra duty around the classroom, or assisting with an art project.

2. Help your child understand why certain actions are considered inappropriate (for example, using foul language is not OK).

3. Explain to your child why the behaviors you are asking him or her to change are not acceptable.

4. Make sure all of your child's teachers understand that they are working on a behavior plan together and they work on developing specific skills together.

5. Ask your child's teachers to give you written feedback or contact them by phone so you can address the behavior issues and come up with solutions that work.

6. Make sure your child is aware that other students are watching their behavior and will let them know if they are doing something wrong.

7. Get family members involved with an incentive plan to help boost your child's self-esteem and confidence while reducing any behavior problems he or she might be having at school or home.

Tips for Managing ADHD Symptoms at School

Sometimes, no matter how much you plan and prepare, and no matter how much work you put into making sure your child's symptoms don't flare up (at school or any other place), bad behaviors might still happen.

It's important to know how to teach your child to manage their symptoms at school, as well as discuss with the teachers how they can help calm down a child with ADHD when things get out of control.

Some tips to keep in mind include:

1. Examine your child's behaviors and see if you can find patterns in their actions, this will help to determine why the behavior is happening in the first place. Take time to recognize your child's behavior and identify what triggers it.

2. Practice self-control methods at home with your child so they can learn how to manage their impulses and focus more easily.

3. Develop a reward system with your child so they understand that behavior has consequences.

4. Use techniques such as positive reinforcement when the child is doing well to encourage them to continue making good choices.

5. Set up a daily schedule, such as going over homework and individual learning challenges with your child every day while reviewing their agenda for the day ahead.

6. Talk to the teachers about creating a Quiet Zone in the classroom area for them to use when they feel they can't focus.

7. Encourage other students and their parents to be aware of the symptoms of ADHD, what triggers them, and how to support the child with ADHD when things get uncontrollable.

8. Be patient with your child and explain that everyone learns differently; some children need more time than others, but everyone will eventually understand as long as they stay focused on the task at hand.

9. Stress the importance of knowing how to self-regulate and calm down when things get out of control.

10. Encourage your child to be involved in sports or other activities that they enjoy so that they can focus on something else entirely instead of being stressed out by schoolwork.

Tips for Making Learning Fun

Learning can be fun, even for a child with ADHD who won't stand still, if you try to keep things organized for them

1. Get your child an agenda that they can carry around to look at between classes.

2. Make sure the agenda contains all of the homework for each class and a calendar to monitor their daily schedule.

3. Be clear about what is expected of your child for the day ahead and how they are expected to manage their time so that they can accomplish everything on time.

Tips for Mastering Homework with an ADHD Child

Although your child might lose focus easily, there are ways to make sure they devote time to their homework (and get it done successfully). One of the things you should do is set aside one hour a day that you plan on working together on their homework and give them as much direction as possible on what they need to do.

Here are some other tips that might help:

1. Develop a routine for doing homework and stick to it with your child every night before bed.

2. If you are not doing the homework yourself, get other family members involved so that your child has support from other caregivers while helping with the homework.

3. Set up a reward system for your child when they complete their homework and use positive reinforcement whenever possible.

4. Talk to the teachers about creating Quiet Zones in the classroom so that your child can get some needed quiet time for them to work on their homework, and also talk with them about how they can provide support in helping your child complete their work or stay focused.

5. Make sure your child has a good night's rest, eats good meals, and exercises regularly so they feel rested the next day.

6. Make sure your child understands the importance of doing their homework right away, and they also know that there are consequences if it's not done.

7. Create a homework routine with your child so they know what to do each night when it is time for them to manage their homework.

8. Set up some quiet time before bed where you can do some studying or reading with your child, read the same book together, or talk about the day ahead

of them tomorrow without any distractions from television, video games, or other activities.

9. If you and your child are struggling with homework that is beyond their ability to manage, let the teacher know. They can give you some tips and support so that you do not get discouraged because of the problem yourself.

10. Make sure your child understands what it takes to do their homework the right way and how long it might take them to finish it. Let them know that they also need time after school to study regularly for them to be successful at school over the long haul.

Helping a Child with ADHD Get Organized

Getting organized is extremely important for your child's education. Some things you might want to do to help your child with this include:

1. Keep a list of supplies necessary for each day's tasks, so the kids know what they'll need and can prepare ahead of time.

2. Create a daily schedule for everything to be completed so that the kids have a good idea of what they need to do each day.

3. Check to ensure that your child has everything they need and that you have everything in place before leaving the house to make sure you don't forget anything important to get home safely.

4. Set up a working space for your child so they know where everything is and how to get things done.

5. Help your child with their homework every day and give them as much support as possible if they are struggling or not sure what to do.

6. Make sure your child understands the importance of organizing themselves and having good time management skills if they want to succeed at school.

7. Keep a daily list of tasks they need to complete each day so that they know exactly what's expected of them when school is over for the day.

8. Help your child with giving themselves structure and routines to help them feel more confident in their abilities and in what they can accomplish if they are committed.

9. Make sure your child understands that being organized can also help others around them so they get things done as well, without any interruptions or issues getting in the way.

10. Set up a reward system for staying organized that your child will appreciate.

Doing all these things will take work, both on your end and from your child's teachers. However, consistency is key, and making sure there's a "system" in

place to help your child manage their ADHD symptoms at school and home will definitely help them succeed in their education!

Chapter 14: Natural Treatment and Remedies for Attention-Deficit/Hyperactivity Disorder

In addition to medication and therapy, you might also want to be aware of some natural treatments and remedies that are known to have helped children with ADHD. In this chapter, we will discuss these alternatives to traditional medication. However, before we dive in, we must also emphasize this: do talk to your doctor about administering any kind of medication to your child (even if it's 100% natural). Only a medical doctor can give you the best advice on these matters, so make sure to discuss with them beforehand.

That being said, let's take a closer look at natural treatments and remedies for ADHD.

Traditional Medication and Side Effects

As we've already mentioned throughout this guide, there are various types of medication for ADHD (such as Ritalin), most of which work by increasing dopamine and norepinephrine in the brain.

Although these medications, when used correctly, provide an effective treatment for children with ADHD, there are several potential side effects that you should be aware of. Some ADHD medications can cause sleep problems, weight gain or loss, mood changes (such as depression or anxiety), and headaches.

Of course, these side effects might sometimes be less significant than letting your child manage their ADHD symptoms on their own, without medication (especially when thinking of the long-term effects of not treating their disorder). However, side effects should be taken into consideration and you should definitely talk to your doctor if you think they are severe.

Food Colorings and Preservatives

Something you should eliminate from your child's diet (and yours, since you want to set a good example) are food colorings and preservatives. The majority of food colorings are artificial, which means they contain chemicals that are not found in nature.

This is a very controversial topic and the scientific evidence in favor of these additives is definitely lacking (or very inconsistent). According to research, artificial food colorants increase hyperactivity and impulsivity when given to children (Arnold, Lofthouse, Hurt, 2012). Fortunately, many natural alternatives exist to these artificial dyes and preservatives (such as beetroot and turmeric), so you don't have to eliminate coloring from your child's foods.

Avoiding Potential Allergens

In some cases, ADHD can be caused by an allergen. Children with hyperactivity symptoms that go away when they take antihistamines may have a food allergy.

The most common allergens are dairy and wheat, but any kind of food can cause a reaction in the right person (so pay close attention to what your child eats).

If you suspect your child has an allergy to a certain food item, make sure to remove it from their diet for up to four weeks and see if their symptoms get better.

EFG Biofeedback

Another option you should look into is EFG Biofeedback (EFT) treatments. These are non-invasive procedures that give the patient biofeedback. In short, this type of treatment entails sending a special electronic signal to the brain and then measuring changes in brain activity.

Some studies have shown that this can help improve ADHD symptoms (by, for example, reducing hyperactivity). However, there isn't enough scientific evidence to support this form of therapy yet, so tread carefully (and discuss it with your doctor before you jump into anything) (Arns et al, 2009).

Yoga and Tai Chi

In addition to the treatments mentioned above, you might be interested in taking a look at various other alternative therapies. Yoga and Tai Chi are two very popular options that have been shown to improve symptoms of ADHD and related problems.

Although there haven't been enough studies on this, many people swear by these techniques. Given that they are completely non-invasive and that, in the worst-case scenario, they will help your child relax and stretch out a little, there's little to lose by trying these techniques (and seeing if they ameliorate ADHD symptoms in your child's situation as well).

Spending Time Outside

Research suggests that outdoor activities can help children with ADHD. In particular, spending time outdoors can increase the amount of dopamine and norepinephrine that the brain produces. Moreover, spending time in nature could lower stress hormones (such as cortisol) and blood pressure levels in people suffering from ADHD.

Behavioral or Parent Therapy

We have already discussed behavioral therapy in previous chapters, but since this too is a non-invasive alternative (or complement) to medication, we mentioned it in this chapter as well. All in all, behavioral therapy has been proven to be one of the single most efficient ways of managing a child with ADHD and helping them cope with their condition in the long run.

Supplements for ADHD Children

There are a variety of different types of supplements used in the treatment of ADHD. Some of these contain choline, caffeine, B vitamins, and other substances (like GABA) that may help alleviate ADHD symptoms.

However, keep in mind that these are not regulated by the FDA and may be ineffective if your child doesn't have an actual deficiency in certain nutrients or vitamins. Even more importantly, DO talk to your doctor before giving your child any kind of supplement, no matter how natural it might be. Just because something is 100% natural, doesn't necessarily mean that it will be beneficial for your child or that it doesn't pose any kind of risk,

Herbal Remedies for ADHD

In addition to actual supplements, some herbal remedies have also been pointed out as helpful in managing ADHD symptoms. Same as in the case of supplements, though, we strongly advise you to discuss these with your doctor before administering them to your child.

Here are some of the most popular ADHD herbal remedies:

- Herbal Tea. Certain types of herbal teas will help calm a child suffering from ADHD. Some of the more popular calming herbal teas include chamomile, peppermint, lavender, valerian, passionflower, and many others.
- Ginkgo Biloba. If you are looking for a natural supplement that can help improve the focus of your child, consider Ginkgo Biloba. It enhances blood flow to the brain and thus can also combat ADHD symptoms.
- Brahmi. Brahmi is a herb that helps lower stress. It is more commonly used in Ayurveda to treat anxiety and depression, but it can also help children with ADHD.

- Gotu Kola. Gotu Kola is another herb that can help improve focus and concentration. It even is helpful for children who suffer from ADHD and are non-verbal (since it enhances their communication skills).
- Green Oats. These are known to help with concentration and focus. It has also been found to improve the memory of those suffering from ADHD.
- Ginseng. This herb is a common remedy used for ADHD in China and other parts of Asia.
- Pine Bark. Pine bark is yet another herbal remedy that can help improve focus and concentration.

Remember: although natural remedies and alternative medicine can provide benefits, the fact that it's not part of the so-called "Big Pharma" doesn't mean it comes without risks. This is precisely why we strongly advise you to take your doctor's advice before giving your child anything that might have side effects (be it a natural treatment or not).

Chapter 15: When Parent and Child Both Have ADHD

As discussed earlier in this book, it's not a rare occurrence that both parents and children suffer from ADHD (genetics being one of the risk factors that could influence the development of this disorder in children). However, it frequently happens that parents do not even know about their ADHD until they have a child, which makes things a little more complicated but, as we keep underlining, not impossible.

In this chapter, we will quickly brush over the main things you should know about situations when both parent(s) and children have ADHD. Although we will not exhaust this topic in one chapter, we do hope to touch upon the main things you should know about this topic.

Moms with ADHD

It is most important to understand that parenting without being aware of ADHD can be extremely difficult for both parent(s) and their child. In general, most children with ADHD are sensitive on one or more levels, and they prefer to stay away from you as much as possible. If you as a parent do not feel that

things are going smoothly, it is a good idea to talk to your child's doctor or consider asking for a consultation with an ADHD specialist.

Being in positions of authority can be especially hard for moms with ADHD since they tend to react more quickly and use more physical force than they should.

Mothers with ADHD often do not become aware of situations that are normal for other people until they start feeling exhausted. The lack of awareness leads to even more stress, which becomes a vicious cycle.

It is important to understand that this kind of behavior — physical fights, ignoring your children's wishes, and ignoring their feelings — does not make any sense as a parent. You must get help for your ADHD symptoms and learn how to communicate with your child in a more appropriate manner.

If you have ADHD and you find that your child is also suffering from it, make sure you do not push him/her into the same habits that started your own ADHD. Instead, try to correct your actions and teach your child in a way that he/she will follow in the future.

Treating Parents with ADHD

If you, as a parent, have been diagnosed with ADHD, you need to seek treatment. The first step would be talking to someone specialized in treating ADHD. It is important to treat both sides of the problem since a change in behavior from one side (parent or child) will affect the other side as well.

However, it is also important to keep in mind that not all parents with ADHD can understand this at first, and some of them tend to reject drugs that treat symptoms associated with ADHD (stimulants). If you happen to find yourself in a similar thought pattern, think of both your well-being and that of your child. Remember, you want to set an example for your child, and following adequate treatments is one of the fundamental things you should do.

In essence, treating an adult with ADHD is not that different from treating a child. Of course, techniques and medication are adapted to the subject's age but, overall, treatment is quite similar.

Chapter 16: ADHD & Emotional Distress Syndrome

As discussed previously, ADHD is frequently associated with comorbid disorders. Emotional Distress Syndrome is among them, and the reason you should know about it is that it can affect both your ADHD child and yourself (as a result of all the stress parenting an ADHD child comes with).

In this chapter, we will quickly discuss what Emotional Distress Syndrome is and how it connects to ADHD. Let's take a look!

Emotional Distress Syndrome: The Basics

Emotional Distress Syndrome is a term coined by James Ochoa, a developmental psychologist, and an ADHD expert with more than 27 years of experience in working with ADHD patients (Ochoa, 2016). Emotional Distress Syndrome refers to a variety of neuropsychiatric disorders that people with ADHD suffer from, such as anxiety disorder, bipolar disorder, depression, substance abuse disorder, and so on.

Emotional Distress Syndrome is more prevalent in children with ADHD than adults with ADHD. Some of the symptoms that usually fall under this syndrome include low self-confidence, overwhelming shame, and guilt, low self-esteem, high levels of anxiety, anger, and resentment, or a tendency to push tasks off on people or things around you.

In general, Emotional Distress Syndrome is a disruptive disorder that can have long-term impacts on the development of the child. It may affect the child's academic achievement, emotional well-being, social interactions, and peer relationships.

Emotional Distress Syndrome is not something that cannot be overcome, though. Same as in the case of ADHD (or any other disorder that affects one's psychological health), treatment and therapy do help.

Overcoming Emotional Distress Syndrome

Some of the most important things to keep in mind when it comes to overcoming Emotional Distress Syndrome include the following tips:

- We all experience struggles in our lives. If you feel ashamed because you are struggling, instead of feeling ashamed, decide to get help via therapy or treatment. You will be able to overcome the disorder if you are willing to work hard and do your part in the effort.
- As mentioned, Emotional Distress Syndrome is not something that cannot be overcome. DO ask for help if you feel overwhelmed, there is ZERO shame in that. This stands just as true for you as it does for your child, and even more so if you or your child are diagnosed with ADHD.
- Keep in mind that overcoming Emotional Distress Syndrome is a long-term affair. You cannot expect to see changes after one session of therapy, but you can expect to see changes if you put in the effort and work on the matters that trouble you.
- Practice mindfulness. Whether it's yoga, meditation, or any other practice rooted in mindfulness, it will help you gain control over your body and mind. In turn, this will help you mitigate symptoms that bother you regularly.

Learn how to relax. Yes, you might be living a very stressful life, but taking time off is essential for your well-being. Deepening yourself in stress and worries will only make your symptoms feel worse, so it's really, really important to take breaks now and again.

Self-Esteem and ADHD

It's easy to see how ADHD could potentially affect one's self-esteem (and how this can, in turn, lead to the development of Emotional Distress Syndrome). ADHD children frequently feel out of place: they cannot stand still, they cannot focus, they perform poorly in school, and they are quite at odds with their social skills as well.

All these things can affect how they see and how they treasure themselves, so as a parent, you should always focus on positive reinforcement. Show your child they are amazing.

They might not do perfectly well in school, and they might have days when it's more difficult to focus on pretty much anything. But as we have shown in previous chapters, there are benefits to ADHD too, so help your child to always focus on those, as opposed to fixating on the things they don't always get right.

Chapter 17: Dealing with an Explosive Child

Children tend to have a lot of energy and that's perfect. It means they are healthy and happy and that they are doing what children do best: exploring the world and learning about it at their own pace (which, let's face it, can be a really speedy one).

Dealing with an explosive child is an entirely different affair though. An ADHD child is not merely energetic, they can be rambunctious, and what's worse, they can end up hurting themselves.

How to deal with an explosive child? Read this chapter to find out more.

Don't Worry Too Much About a Diagnosis

You will meet many well-meaning people on your child's road to diagnosis. Many will be doctors but others may be teachers, psychologists, speech therapists, and many other professionals. These are the people who will be your allies in the fight for your child's treatment plan through their guidance and advice.

You could also meet some less well-meaning people including school administrators, social workers, and teachers. They may show little to no understanding of what ADHD means, and more than that, they may show little to no interest in ever learning about it.

What is important, however, is to hold your ground. A diagnosis is just that: a name on a page that theoretically helps medical professionals and therapists find better solutions. Beyond that, however, what is truly essential is to help your child get their behavior under control and show them how to manage themselves when their symptoms are flaring.

Explosive Children May Lack Some Cognitive Skills

Keep in mind that explosive children are not just overly energetic. They might lack important cognitive skills that help them regulate their energy levels, attention, focus, and learning capabilities. That is precisely why it is SO important for you as a parent to teach these skills to your child and show them "the way."

For instance, self-awareness is a very important skill children with ADHD should learn.

What is self-awareness? It's the key to having a positive relationship with yourself. If you don't know how you act in certain situations and what triggers those reactions, it's really hard to react positively.

Expectations Outstrip Skills

Explosive children tend to have very high expectations of themselves. They tend to think they are capable of more than what they are actually able to deliver. As a result, explosive children regularly let themselves down as well as disappoint their parents.

The reason for this is that explosive children are often not as capable as they think and may act before thinking while lacking the cognitive skills necessary for their daily lives.

It is important to help your child manage their expectations when it comes to the skills they have and the skills they still have to work on. Of course, you want to show them as much positive reinforcement as possible, but only when the situation requires it. Do not lie to your child saying they're doing well with something they aren't, but emphasize the things they are doing well on and the things they are slowly mastering.

Figure out Your Child's Specific Situation

Not all ADHD children are the same. Some may be more focused in certain situations, some may be completely hyperactive in other situations. Figuring out which skills your child lacks and which expectations they are not managing properly is essential for their development precisely because it will help you, the parent, guide them in the right direction.

Try a New Parenting Plan

Gone are the days when you could treat the symptoms of your child's ADHD and hope things get better. While a diagnosis may help you identify some of the underlying causes, it doesn't simply mean that you can wait for your child to learn on their own.

Once you get a diagnosis, it is essential to figure out a new parenting plan that will bring more structure into your child's daily life. And if that parenting plan doesn't show the expected results, you should be prepared to adopt a new parenting plan. Change and adjustments are frequently required, so mentally prepare yourself for some fine-tuning in how you parent your child.

Solve Problems Proactively

Explosive children tend to be reactive when it comes to solving problems. They tend to react after they have already made a mess of things and then they explode.

What you need is a proactive solution — something that preemptively prevents the situation from reaching the explosion point and that teaches your child how to solve problems before they are faced with an explosive situation.

Prioritize Problems Before Solving Them

There is a great difference between explosive children and other children when it comes to problem-solving. Explosive children will have a tendency to attempt solving problems in a very freeform manner.

They will usually tackle all kinds of different problems as long as they are excited about doing so while neglecting other problems that could be more important or more urgent.

You need to prioritize the problems your child has and work on fixing them one at a time without allowing your child to distract themselves with smaller, less important issues or tasks.

The same applies to how you tackle your child's skills as well. Is it more important for them to make eye contact with other kids or to keep them focused for more than three minutes at a time? Focus on the things that affect your child more directly and which could have a long-lasting effect and tackle those first. Then, move on to other skills.

Don't Mislabel Your Child

Remember that your child suffers from a disorder that affects them in more ways than one. They are not just simply naughty or rascals, their brains are just not wired to focus or stay put, and that makes it hard for them to perform well in a vast array of situations (school included).

Do not mislabel your child by thinking they are simply naughty or difficult when, in reality, you may be overreacting to their situation.

If you think that is the case, then enlist the help of a professional who will be able to find out if your child's ADHD affects more of their behavior than you can see. Otherwise, you might end up focusing more on your child's misbehavior than on helping them deal with the root cause of their issues.

Get Good at Plan B

Parenting, in general, is all about being very good at making plans...lots of them, for the same matter. Parenting an explosive child means you have to be even better at building plan B, plan C, plan D...and so on.

With explosive children, you have to be ready to adjust your plans a great deal, prioritizing what's most important and what could be dealt with easily. At the same time, you also need to make sure that these other plans are not just discarded along the way as it is more likely they will come in handy later on. Get

good at building contingency plans and build in an unforeseen problem for later on.

Don't Fret Over Disagreements

If your child refuses to eat or they throw a tantrum at the dinner table, don't worry about it. They may not be hungry and they are probably just tired. They may want to go to bed or something else and you shouldn't force them to do anything they don't wish for. Don't insist on disagreeing and constantly fighting with your child -- it won't do them any good, and it will most certainly not benefit you either.

Indeed, raising an overly active child can be a challenge, but it does come with a good dose of positives as well. Focus on those whenever times get tough and then roll back your sleeves to be the parent your child needs you to be: one who knows how to guide them through the perpetually-distracting world "out there."

Chapter 18: Possible Casualties of Parenting an Explosive Child

Staying positive is always important and even more so when you are parenting a child with ADHD. However, that doesn't mean you shouldn't be prepared for the worst-case scenarios too — which is precisely what we will discuss in this chapter. Read on if you want to learn more about the possible casualties of parenting an explosive child.

Your Relationship with Your Child

Sometimes, parenting a child with ADHD requires a bit of toughness. And other times, it requires you to be as soft as a human can be. All these shifts, as well as the rather rigid life you will organize around your child's life can have

an impact on how they perceive you (now, as well as when they grow up into teenagers, and then into adults).

Be prepared for a relationship that might not always look bright.

Your Relationship with Yourself

How you feel during the six months after your child is diagnosed with ADHD can affect how well you handle the frustration and stress of parenting a child with ADHD. The stronger your relationship was during the time leading up to diagnosis, the better your ability to overcome this adversity becomes.

There is no magic formula for building a strong relationship with your child before he is diagnosed; however, you can build a stronger connection as time goes on. And even more than that, you can build yourself into a stronger person (trust us, you WILL need this).

Do not blame yourself for what is happening. All the planning in the world cannot determine whether or not a child will develop ADHD, so there's really no reason to feel guilty over this. Practice self-love and gratitude, instead -- they will be a lot more helpful.

Your Relationship with Your Spouse or Partner

We get it: parenting with ADHD often doesn't make things easier at home. You may feel like you are battling against the entire world and that's okay! Family life is never easy when there is an ADHD child in it -- as we know all too well.

Make sure both you and your partner are on the same page in terms of parenting methods, behavioral cues, and techniques. Also, be sure you are both mentally strong to withstand what's coming towards you. Don't neglect your own relationship, either, because sooner or later, one of you will end up bitter and remorseful — that will not help anyone, not you, not your child.

Your Relationships with Your Other Children

Having a child with ADHD can cause some pretty dramatic changes in your other children's lives, not to mention their emotions.

For example, did you know that children with an ADHD sibling are significantly more likely to have emotional disorders as well? And that includes depression!

The good news is that your relationship with your other children will be strengthened if you treat them fairly. If you can do this, then there is a good

chance they will learn from your lessons and rise above the challenges themselves.

Your Friendships

It happens: out of necessity, you will be spending more time with your child than with your friends.

And while we are all for enjoying time spent with your child (it is definitely a good idea to make sure they occupy your time), don't neglect the people who love you and were there for you during the other times of the year!

Our relationships with other people are what keep us grounded, and you don't want to lose that or be left without a friend when you need them most. Take care of your friendships as much as you take care of your marital relationship and your relationship with your child. They might not seem as important in the grand scheme of things, but they are the "check-in" everyone needs — including parents of ADHD children!

The Ideas You Once Had of "Normal"

Your definition of "normal" will severely alter over the coming years, and you need to acknowledge that. Accept it as it is and embrace the "new normal," there is no other solution. After a while, you will learn to not only accept this new kind of normality but truly appreciate it as well. Because what parent doesn't love the idea of a very happy, energetic kid?

The Resemblance to the Parent You Thought You Would Be

As we have mentioned, parenting with ADHD can take a toll on you. One of the ways you can change this is by altering your perception of yourself as a parent.

Here's what we mean: to be a good parent you must be willing to do anything for your child. Even if this means going against everything you previously believed in regarding parenting techniques and strategies (e.g., playdates, consistent rules, and consequences, etc.).

Your Ability to See Yourself as a Capable Strong Parent

This is one of the most important parts of your journey. You must be able to see yourself as a strong and capable parent.

If you don't, then you will have a hard time making your relationship with your child work. The only thing that can get you through the next six months is seeing yourself as the best parent possible. However, if you want to go beyond this, start by admitting that this was not something that was planned for you, and that's okay.

Be prepared for everything, because this will allow you to create plans and take preemptive actions before things get completely out of control. You have a lot of bumps in your road, and nobody can deny that. The good news is that there is SO much information out there on how to be a good parent to an ADHD child! Sure, you will have to learn how to sift through the "fake news," but once you get a hang of that, you will discover the world is a pretty supportive place for people like you, so you will always find solutions to your problems.

Chapter 19: Emotional Development in Childhood

You don't have to get a psychology degree to be a good parent, not even when you are parenting a child with ADHD (or any other disorder). However, learning more about how your child will develop will help you create the right environment for them. Remember that parenting a child with ADHD can be significantly different than parenting other children, so knowing about their emotional development becomes even more important.

It is precisely for this reason that we chose to dedicate a chapter entirely to this: how children develop emotionally in their first years of life (and why this is important for ADHD parenting).

Let's dig deeper and look at the skills and behaviors considered normal for kids in every age group.

From 0 to 12 Months

When kids are born, they are often referred to as "temperamental." They have very strong, contradictory emotions and don't know how to deal with their feelings.

They express negative emotions more easily than positive ones, which makes them unpleasant to be around for anyone who doesn't want them as a friend. Because they have many of the same emotions as an adult, their expressions can be really confusing — for example, when they are fussy and crying and no one knows why.

Babies also have a self-soothing "mechanism," and they are at a phase where they are still learning a lot about the world (including how to differentiate facial expressions, for example). It is an age of marvel and discovery that borders on a miracle.

From 12 Months to 2 Years

From the time your child is one to two years old, you will start to notice that they can recognize their emotions more easily. They've also developed the ability to regulate them and keep their impulses in check.

They're capable of seeing things from other people's perspectives without completely losing touch with their own point of view. This is true empathy: recognition of another person's feelings based on your own perspective, without losing yourself entirely.

From 2 to 5 Years

The period from 2 to 5 is a time when children develop social skills. They will be able to read your moods and emotions and react accordingly.

They will start to develop self-control around the age of 4, but they will just have a "conscious" understanding of what this means and how it works.

Around the age of 5, kids also start to develop a conscience — it is at this point that they start feeling guilty after doing something wrong.

From 5 to 7 Years

The 5-7 years old period is one of the big changes in terms of emotional development.

Your child will start to read their parents' facial expressions and emotions better, and they will start to learn how to make friends. They will understand the world better and be more able to consider other people's points of view.

They will also develop a greater sense of control over their impulses, which can help them avoid acting impulsively.

From 7 to 10 Years

This is a period in which kids develop their capacity to show sympathy to others. They will also be better able to consider others' perspectives and understand how their actions affect other people.

From 10 to 13 Years

This is also a time of great changes in emotional development. Your child will be more able to identify their feelings and recognize other people's feelings. They will have a deeper understanding of how their actions affect other people.

They will also be able to manage their emotions better. Parents should make sure that they understand the meaning of words like anxiety, stress, and depression so they can express themselves and get help when needed.

From 13 Years Onwards

Your child will continue to develop into an adult, both emotionally and socially. They will have better emotional control and be able to make better decisions.

Though this period is often overlooked in families, it's a very important one for your child's development (and how they will behave as adults later on in life). Although at this point your child might be more independent, it is important to acknowledge that they might still need your help (even if they don't specifically ask for it). As a parent, you will have to find the fine balance between offering to help and allowing your child to learn how to stand on their own feet.

Keep in mind that these stages of emotional development are quite standard, but that doesn't mean that all children follow the same patterns. In the case of a child with ADHD, it is important to help them build on what's normal for them. They may never be able to be as social as other children, but you can

help them find balance and be as efficient as possible at acquiring friends and building steady relationships, for example.

You cannot expect things to happen to the textbook in the case of a child with ADHD. But you CAN expect them to eventually develop healthy emotions and ways of coping with their emotions from multiple points of view.

Chapter 20: Mood Disorders in Children and Adolescents with ADHD

Mood disorders are a special category of disorders, which are very commonly associated with children that have ADHD. Some children develop these mood disorders in childhood, together with their ADHD, while others develop them in their adolescence or even adulthood.

Knowing about these disorders will help you spot issues early and give your child the help they need, so we dedicated a chapter to this topic as well.

Let's dive into it!

What Are Mood Disorders?

Mood disorders are mental health disorders that involve mood disturbances and changes in your child's overall emotions. Some mood disorders include things like depression, anxiety, or bipolar disorder. Depression is maybe the most common of these mood disorders, and it typically entails the presence of depressive episodes.

Depression is different from just feeling sad, as it is a mental illness that includes some serious changes in terms of symptoms. Depressive episodes can

involve feelings like hopelessness, sadness, anger, agitation or irritability, poor concentration levels, and fatigue.

Children with ADHD are at risk of developing mood disorders, including depression, bipolar disorder, and dysthymic disorder (which is a low-grade depression connected to feelings of hopelessness and low self esteem). All of these mental health problems are very serious and you should not treat them as passing moods, but conditions that can affect your child's quality of life now and in the future as well.

Suspected Causes

It is not known why children with ADHD are at risk of developing mood disorders. However, some common factors might play a role in this.

For example, children with ADHD often display symptoms of depression when they are under extreme stress or have a lot on their plates. This is because the symptoms of ADHD pose a threat to their relationships with other people and their ability to perform well in school.

Furthermore, children with ADHD tend to have low self-esteem and a destructive relationship with the world, which can lead to increased feelings of anxiety. This is because parents of children with ADHD are frequently criticized about their parenting skills or about their child's behavior.

Last but not least, children with ADHD often feel the pressure to succeed in a crowd of high-achievers. Lack of sleep is another common issue affecting children and adolescents with ADHD, so they may develop an unhealthy relationship between problems, sleeping, and mood disorders.

Signs and Symptoms

Children with ADHD can develop mood disorders that are connected to depression, bipolar disorder, or dysthymia. The symptoms of these disorders include feelings of hopelessness and despair, loss of interest in activities that you used to enjoy, an overall lack of energy and motivation, sleep disturbances (for example insomnia), problems with focus and concentration, and a negative outlook on life.

Diagnosis

A doctor will perform a simple examination to check whether your child has depression or other mood disorders. They will also ask you more specific

questions about your child's thoughts, opinions, and feelings regarding things like schoolwork, friends and family issues, social activities, etc.

In some cases, a mental health professional may also assess the presence of ADHD and make additional recommendations for treatment if necessary.

Treatment

Children with ADHD often have difficulty accepting that they have a problem that requires treatment (and adults suffering from these conditions may display a similar behavior as well). However, once open, they find there are many treatment options.

For example, they can be prescribed certain medications to help them deal with their depression and other mood disorders. Another option may be a combination of medication and psychotherapy or cognitive behavior therapy. These two treatment approaches can be very beneficial, as can supportive environments in which children with ADHD and mood disorders can slow down and focus on themselves for a while.

Sometimes, it is "at home" techniques that make a big difference. For instance, encouraging a mood journal for your child or teen to understand more about their feelings and what triggers their mood changes.

Individual Therapy

None of these mood disorders go away on their own. As mentioned above, these are not passing moods, but issues that persist and can affect one's life to the point of degrading it completely. You definitely do not want this for your child, so it is important to show them therapy is essential in finding better ways to cope with their thoughts and emotions.

There are multiple therapeutic approaches for people suffering from mood disorders, including behavioral therapy (but not only). Your child might have to go through some of them until they find the one that works best for their specific situation.

Medication Options

Medication is a frequent option in treating mood disorders. However, some issues come with this. Most of the medication used to treat mood disorders may have side effects such as insomnia, weight gain, nausea, irritability, and depression.

The good news is that there are many alternatives to these medications. For example, there are drug-free approaches such as nutrients (like magnesium), light therapy, and exercise; all of them influence the level of neurotransmitters in the brain which control your emotions.

If, however, your child's doctor prescribes medication, it is important to heed them and administer them to your child. Likewise, it is not recommended to give your child any kind of supplements before checking with your physician first (you don't want to do more harm than good, right?).

Treating ADHD and its comorbid disorders (including mood disorders) is not a one-size-fits-all recipe. This is precisely why your child might have to go through several attempts and combinations of treatments until they find something that is truly efficient for them. Be patient, and teach them to be patient as well: solutions *will* be found and they *will* grow into harmonious adults.

Chapter 21: Build Your Child's Self Esteem

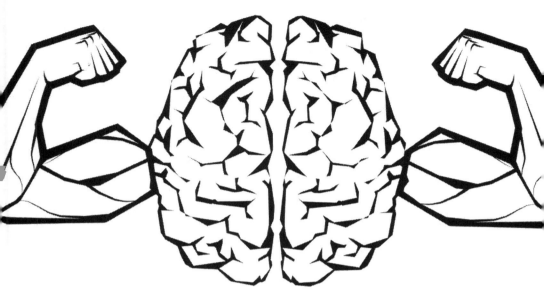

Nobody is perfect. Your child just happens to have a diagnosis for the things that make them less than perfect (but absolutely amazing at the same time). Teaching your child to accept who they are and what are their pluses and minuses is essential for them to develop healthily and harmoniously — helping them build their self-esteem is a crucial part of all this.

How to build your child's self-esteem? Here are some tips you might want to remember (Hallowell, Jensen, 2021).

The 5-Step Plan to Build Your Child's Self Esteem

OK, as we were discussing earlier in the book at hand, there's no one-size-fits-all kind of solution to parenting a child with ADHD. But if you have to narrow it down into an actionable plan, the 5-step plan is one of the best solutions to build your child's self-esteem.

Where does this plan start?

It starts with you and your positive parenting. Knowing your child beyond their diagnosis is essential here because it will allow you to capture their true spirit: the traits that have little to do with their diagnosis, but who they are as (tiny, for now) human beings.

Build Self Esteem: Create a Connected Childhood

Once you know your child's basics (their strengths and weaknesses, as well as their natural personality traits), you can start building their self-esteem by helping them to feel connected to the world around them.

This means that you will have to create a culture of positivity around your child: a place where they can develop confidence in themselves, based on something meaningful.

You don't have to be an expert on positive parenting; all you need is to be consistent and patient with them. A connected childhood is not a picture-perfect, Hollywood-polished one, but one in which the child has a healthy connection to you, allowing them to always come back to a safe space in their minds and hearts where they can ground themselves and feel at ease.

Build Self Esteem: Encourage Play

When you know what your child's strengths and weaknesses are, you can also start to encourage them to develop a connection with things that are made for children, such as play.

This is because play is a way for kids to explore their emotions and identify their qualities and characteristics. Playing with other children is the most effective tool to boost confidence and build self-esteem in children.

Your child's social skills may not be great right now. However, with your help, your child can definitely make friends. All they need is the right environment and opportunities to start connecting with others, and you will have to be the one to create these opportunities.

Last, but not least, make sure that your child gets out of the house often — this can be either by enrolling them into daycare or summer camps or by scheduling activities with other families through playdates and group sessions.

Build Self Esteem: Help Them Master a Problem

Now that your child has a solid connection with the world around him, he can start looking at himself with a more critical eye. And this is when the spotlight is on you again — more specifically on the way you handle his challenges.

When it comes to helping your child build self-esteem, one of the ways to do so is by helping them master a problem. This will allow them to develop skills that they can use to confront other similar situations in their lives. Not only will it make their lives easier (and yours), but it will also help your child trust their own capabilities more.

Build Self Esteem: Give Recognition

This is one of the most important steps in building your child's self-esteem. The goal is to reward your child when they master certain tasks, thereby increasing their confidence and motivating them to move forward.

Think about it this way: when you reward something that takes effort, you are praising it and acknowledging its importance. You are also reinforcing the fact that it is worth doing for a reason — that reason will require them to work on their skills, see results, and grow in their sense of worthiness and confidence.

Aside from the five-step plan to building self-esteem, you might also want to keep in mind the following tips:

Be an Encouraging Parent

If there's one thing you should keep in mind while working on building your child's self-esteem, it's this: Be an encouraging parent.

In other words, make them feel good about their accomplishments. They don't have to be significant ones — and they shouldn't be necessary, either — but the way you compliment them goes a long way.

Build your child's confidence as a parent by showing genuine support for your child.

It's one thing to say "Good job!" but another to go a step further and be proud of what they accomplished, which will then encourage them to try even harder.

Get Your Child Involved in Activities

When you think about building your child's self-esteem, you must get them involved in some form of physical activity. Doing this will not only help them tame down the energy "monster" inside of them, but it will also help them regulate their emotions and body image (especially as they grow up).

Remember that Feedback IS Important

It's one thing to be an encouraging parent and it's a completely different matter to close your eyes when your child is doing something that's not right (for them or others). As mentioned earlier in the book, discuss things with your child when they misbehave and do it as soon as possible, don't wait for "later". You have to learn how to find the right words and tone for these kinds of discussions not to affect the little ones, but they are still essential for the harmonious development of your child.

Find Balance in Your Own Authority

Remember that you, as a parent, have an immense influence on the development of your child's self-esteem (due to your authority and power), but this doesn't mean that you should use it whenever possible. This is why you need to be honest about your child's accomplishments and remember to give feedback when they do something wrong or bad.

Maybe this is easier said than done — maybe it's not always easy to find the right words — but it is one of the most important things when building self-esteem in children.

Of course, these are not the ONLY ways to build self-esteem in a child (with or without ADHD). However, these basics will hopefully help you understand why self-esteem is so important and how you can help your child be more balanced.

Chapter 22: Toys and Games for Kids with ADHD

Play is of the utmost importance in the development of any child, and someone diagnosed with ADHD isn't an exception to the rule. However, since you want your child's toys and games to help him develop skills (and not be more distracting), you will have to learn how to select the best options for them.

What are some tips when it comes to toys and games for kids with ADHD? Read on and find out more.

Fantasy Toys for the Younger Kids

A very young child diagnosed with ADHD might have a hard time understanding what's going on. This is precisely why at this age, toys must act as a support in developing skills that help them discover the world (and beyond it). Opt for fantasy toys that will provide an imaginary but safe environment for your child to play in.

Encourage Them to Continue

Games where your child has to complete the story, puzzles, and similar games that allow them to focus on the storyline in front of them are extremely helpful. These games enable your child to learn more about causality and how actions should flow in a normal rhythm (or, well, as normal as fantasy play allows).

Rehearsing Social Behaviors

Another game you can play with your child is rehearsing different social behaviors you want them to acquire. For example, be the one to introduce your child to holding hands, practicing eye contact, and other important social indicators. Although these skills are harder to master in fantasy play situations, it is a good idea to start them while they're young.

Social-Emotional Games

Games that help your child practice social skills should be the first ones that spring into mind when you're shopping for toys and games for kids with ADHD. However, games that deal with more social-emotional aspects of their lives should also be considered. Introduce your child to board games focused on life dilemmas and other similar situations.

Furthermore, when it comes to choosing toys for kids with ADHD, it is also worthwhile to look into social stories – one of the best tools when it comes to teaching them about emotions and how they fit into everyday life.

Keep It Simple

Same as with everything in the life of a child with ADHD, games, and toys should be kept simple. If they are too intricate and complex, your child might lose focus, become anxious, and throw a tantrum. The simpler your games are, the easier they will pick it up, stay engaged, and use play to acquire important skills.

Teaching Responsibility

If you play a game with your child where you have to take care of a certain object (maybe even a person, if you have really little ones), you can use this time to teach them the basics of taking responsibility. For example, make sure your child is putting their toys back into the box or their dolls into the house after playtime, and praise them for this. Doing this will help them develop great life habits and practice responsibility at an early age.

Aside from the tips mentioned above, do keep in mind that the best games and toys are those in which you are both involved. Your child loves to spend time with you and you, as the parent, are the one who will teach them all these skills that are more difficult for them. So why not do it in a fun way, which the child can associate with positive emotions, rather than the stress and pressure of a classroom or organized homework session?

Of course, classrooms, homework, and organization are all crucial but don't forget to sprinkle your parenting with some good, old-fashioned play. It can do wonders, both for you and for your child!

Conclusion

According to a national parent survey run in 2016, more than 6 million children have ever been diagnosed with ADHD in the United States of America. And that's just the cases that are diagnosed, as there are definitely many others out there (CDC, 2021).

Attention Deficit Hyperactivity Disorder is not just a diagnosis that is made because of a lack of focus. It is more accurately described as a developmental disorder that can be triggered by many different factors which can have tremendous effects on a child's life.

Our main goal with the book at hand was, from the get-go, to give you an introduction to what is a very complex topic: parenting an overly energetic child. We hope that the information we provided in this guide has given you a better idea of what to do next if your child has been diagnosed with ADHD (or if the diagnosis is still pending).

In all honesty, aside from information, the one thing you should acquire (and SOON!) is patience. If your child was diagnosed with ADHD, you must understand the condition. Not insisting on immediate action may be the right thing to do, but it is also important to not spend too much time in this "limbo." The sooner you develop a clear plan, the better off your child will be in the end.

Furthermore, you need to understand that ADHD is not just a fancy name for overly energetic kids. Yes, kids have energy. And yes, that is absolutely lovely. However, some kids have far more energy than is normal, and that can be a very problematic occurrence.

The good news is that there are things you can do to help your child manage their "excess energy." It's not easy, and it will require some work on your part (which circles us back to the word "patience" we have just mentioned above).

Every parent wants their child to be the best, brightest, and most successful human in history, and you probably don't make much of an exception here. An ADHD diagnosis doesn't have to come with disillusionment and pain though. It can be the exact thing that pushes both you and your child forward, precisely because they have to work twice as hard as everyone else to acquire skills other children find just... easy.

Moreover, as shown in one of our chapters here, there are benefits to ADHD. While this disorder might come with a lot of chaos, it can also come with a lot of creativity, drive, and energy -- qualities that are quite common among the single most successful artists, musicians, athletes, and even politicians and business people.

YES, your child can and will succeed. It's just that you have to adjust your parenting style to this disorder, which may sometimes mean that you'll need to

learn for yourself how to keep your cool, and how to make sure you are the best parent your child could ever have.

Celebrate and bask in the energy bomb your child is, really. It's FAR better to have a child who runs around happily all the time than a child who doesn't know the joy of life from a very young age. And while your child's energy might get them in trouble sometimes, it can also be the fuel that makes them shine bright like diamonds as they develop into fully functional, healthy, balanced adults.

Before we close this book, there is one more thing we need to emphasize again: take care of yourself too. Raising an explosive child can deplete all your energy, so it is absolutely crucial that you take breaks regularly. You don't expect your phone to go on forever on a single charge, so why would you expect your mental and physical health to be any other way?

We understand your child is your number one priority, but that doesn't mean you should ever neglect yourself. Doing so will benefit nobody: not you, not your spouse or life partner, not your friends, not your career, and most definitely not your child.

Just think of it: do you think your child needs an exhausted parent? How will you ever help them if your own batteries are perpetually depleted? You might feel like a bad parent having to take a break every now and again, but the absolute truth is that you need this just as much as you need nourishment, sleep, and water.

A lot of parents (and not just those raising ADHD children) put themselves last in an effort to dedicate all their energy to their children. However, this is unhealthy, especially in the long run. Not only will it set a bad example for children (and particularly ADHD children), but it can also make you more irritable, and it can lead to the development of further medical issues (both mental and physical).

Taking breaks is not only good for you but also necessary. I cannot emphasize this enough. The journey ahead of you is not an easy one and *nobody* can run marathons back to back for too long. Your body and your mind need rest, so *please* do take care of yourself.

Keep a positive attitude, as much as possible. There are some bumpy times ahead of you, but focusing on the bright side will help you overcome them. And most importantly, it will help you be the parent your child needs you to be: one who constantly underlines the fact that the glass is half full.

Focusing on the bad sides will only yield more negativity — you definitely don't need that in your life (even more so through the perspective of trying to set a healthy example for your own child).

Good luck in your parenting journey, I truly hope the book at hand has proved useful!

References

American Psychiatric Association. (2021). *What is obsessive-compulsive disorder?* Psychiatry.org. https://www.psychiatry.org/patients-families/ocd/what-is-obsessive-compulsive-disorder.

Arnold, L., Lofthouse, N. and Hurt, E.. (2012). *Artificial food colors and attention-deficit/hyperactivity symptoms: Conclusions to dye for.* Neurotherapeutics, 9(3), pp.599-609.

Arns, M., de Ridder, S., Strehl, U., Breteler, M. and Coenen, A. (2009). *Efficacy of neurofeedback treatment in ADHD: The effects on inattention, impulsivity and hyperactivity: A meta-Analysis.* Clinical EEG and Neuroscience, 40(3), pp.180-189.

Bhandari, S. (2019). *Nonstimulants and other ADHD drugs.* WebMD. https://www.webmd.com/add-adhd/adhd-nonstimulant-drugs-therapy

CDC. (2021). *Data and statistics about ADHD.* Centers for Disease Control and Prevention. https://www.cdc.gov/ncbddd/adhd/data.html

CDC. (2021). *Data and statistics about ADHD.* Centers for Disease Control and Prevention. https://www.cdc.gov/ncbddd/adhd/data.html

CHADD. (2021). *ADHD and long-term outcomes.* https://chadd.org/about-adhd/long-term-outcomes/.

CHADD. (2021). *Tics and tourette syndrome.* https://chadd.org/about-adhd/tics-and-tourette-syndrome.

Cram. (2021). *Behavior therapy by B. F. Skinner's goals and methods.* Cram.com. https://www.cram.com/essay/Behavior-Therapy-By-B-F-Skinners-Goals/F3SSNJ5KGZKQ.

Faraone, S. and Larsson, H. (2019). Genetics of attention deficit hyperactivity disorder. Molecular Psychiatry, 24, pp.562–575.

Hallowell, E. and Jensen, P. (2021). *The ADHD soul shine kit: Build your child's self esteem.* ADDitude. https://www.additudemag.com/self-esteem-build-adhd-child-confidence/

Healthline. (2020). *14 signs of ADHD: Does your child have ADHD?.* Healthline. https://www.healthline.com/health/adhd/signs#lack-of-focus.

Healthline. (2021). *What's bipolar disorder? How do I know if I have it?.* Healthline. https://www.healthline.com/health/bipolar-disorder

Healthline. (2021). *Why having ADHD can be a benefit.* Healthline. https://www.healthline.com/health/adhd/benefits-of-adhd.

Kessler, E. (2021). *Dr. Amen's 7 types of ADHD.* Smart Kids. https://www.smartkidswithld.org/getting-help/adhd/7-types-adhd/.

Mayo Clinic. (2021). *Oppositional defiant disorder (ODD) - Symptoms and causes.* https://www.mayoclinic.org/diseases-conditions/oppositional-defiant-disorder/symptoms-causes/syc-20375831

NHS. (2021). *Attention deficit hyperactivity disorder ADHD.* https://www.nhs.uk/conditions/attention-deficit-hyperactivity-disorder-adh

Ochoa, J. (2016). Free webinar replay: *Emotional distress syndrome and the ADHD brain.* ADDitude. https://www.additudemag.com/webinar/emotional-distress-syndrome-adhd-brain/

Ratini, M. (2020). *Tic disorders and twitches.* WebMD. https://www.webmd.com/brain/tic-disorders-and_twitches

Robinson, L., Smith, M., A, M., Segal, J. and Ramsey, D. (2020). *ADHD medications - HelpGuide.org.* HelpGuide.org. https://www.helpguide.org/articles/add-adhd/medication-for-attention-deficit-disorder-adhd.htm#

Silver, L. (2019). *ADHD medication side effects no one should tolerate.* ADDitude. https://www.additudemag.com/adhd-medication-side-effects-that-no-one-should-tolerate/.

Singer, E. (2007). *A neurological basis for ADHD.* MIT Technology Review. https://www.technologyreview.com/2007/08/09/224410/a-neurological-basis-for-adhd.

Usami, M. (2016). Functional consequences of attention-deficit hyperactivity disorder on children and their families. Psychiatry and Clinical Neurosciences, 70(8), pp.303-317.

Made in the USA
Las Vegas, NV
29 November 2022